Hiding Behind A Mask

LIVING MED FREE FROM DEPRESSION & BIPOLAR II DISORDER

Cheryl Bolton Van Winkle

Endorsements

Cheryl suffered from bipolar two depression for over 40 years. She was on antidepressants for 17 years. Cheryl and her husband were pastors and learned that many in the faith community failed to understand the depth of her pain. Ultimately, she learned that God wanted to do more than remove the depression, He wanted her whole.

To all who love truth, Cheryl Van Winkle tells a compelling story of healing and deliverance from depression. Her book offers a balance between good Christian medical care and spiritual healing. She shows that there is no quick fix for the heaviness of depression. Rather, healing from depression is a journey. Cheryl has made the journey and her book offers hope to all who suffer from this malady.

Dr. Ron Phillips
Senior Pastor
Abba's House Hixson, TN

This moving story challenges Christians to become better educated about clinical depression and to move from labeling and judgment to understanding, encouragement and love. If you or a loved one struggle with depression, Cheryl's story will give you hope and practical advice. She challenges you to visit those hard places of your heart and invite God to soften them--His Light dispels darkness. Let her "spark" ignite fire in you. After all, God is still in the miracle working business!

Rujon Morrison
Co Founder, Healing for the Nations
Marietta, GA

When we first met Cheryl, and her husband David, they were "young and upwardly mobile". We were privileged to be their pastors; we also became friends. When God called them into ministry, a journey began in their lives that would impact so many others. Yet, Cheryl suffered - sometimes at the hands of those she was called to minister to, sometimes from the poor counsel of those attempting to find the answers to her plaguing problems. Cheryl and David are survivors. They did not give up. They found answers. Hopefully, these answers will be a help to you whether you are the sufferer or the one who seeks to relieve the suffering.

Pastors Dan & Sharon Estes
Trinity Assembly of God
Georgetown, KY

For Booking information
contact the author at:

cherylbvanwinkle@gmail.com

Facebook.com/Cheryl.b.vanwinkle
www.cherylvanwinkle.myqsciences.com for product
information and purchases.

The author welcomes your comments about this book. Email
to let her know what you found helpful.

DISCLAIMER: Cheryl Bolton Van Winkle is not a physician and
does not intend to be giving medical advice by anything that
she says in this book to the reader. It is strongly advised that you
consult your physician before changing or discontinuing your
medication or before you begin fasting. Neither the publisher
nor the author is responsible for any possible consequences from
any person reading or following the information in this book.

All Scripture quotations are taken from the King James Version of
the Bible.

Copyright 2011 by Cheryl Bolton Van Winkle

All rights reserved

ISBN : 0-615-43698-6
ISBN : 13:978-0-615-43698-2
LCCN: 2011900404

Second Edition
Printed in the United States of America
Cheryl Bolton VanWinkle, Eustis, Florida

I dedicate this book to my Lord and Savior Jesus Christ, who has walked with me throughout my journey to find health and wholeness.

CONTENTS

INTRODUCTION
Why I Wrote This Book..i
1. A Cold Winter Day   1
2. Growing Up In Kentucky.....................................7
3. The Accident 23
4. A New Love..31
5. Born Again 39
6. Postpartum Depression 43
7. The Call..49
8. Good News 57
9. Diagnosis Bi-polar Two....................................69
10. A Way of Escape...81
11. Proper Diagnosis 93
12. Signs of Depression 101
13. SAD-Seasonal Affective Disorder..........................113
14. Laser Light Therapy 117
15. Genetics and Depression..................................121
16. Words Cause Depression...................................127
17. Living With Someone Who Is Depressed.....................137
18. Depression Among Teens...................................149
19. How I Received Supernatural Healing......................157
20. More Scriptures Regarding Healing 179
21. Update! Finally Med Free!!! 199

To appoint unto them that mourn in Zion, to give unto them beauty for ashes, the oil of joy for mourning, the garment of praise for the spirit of heaviness; that they might be called trees of righteousness, the planting of the LORD, that he might be glorified.

Isaiah 61:3

INTRODUCTION

୶୷

Why I Wrote This Book

¹The Spirit of the Lord GOD is upon me; because the LORD hath anointed me to preach good tidings unto the meek; he hath sent me to bind up the brokenhearted, to proclaim liberty to the captives, and the opening of the prison to them that are bound. (Isaiah 61:1)

For most of my life, I have heard people who were well meaning; criticize people who were suffering from depression. Recently, a famous TV pastor said, "When I hear someone say they want prayer for depression, a spirit of slap comes all over me." He said, "They say that depression is caused from a chemical imbalance, but I think the chemical imbalance is caused from the depression." As a child growing up with a mother and grandmother who suffered from what I now recognize as chronic, debilitating bipolar depression, I used to feel the same way until I took a long walk in their shoes.

Even my mother's so called best friend told my father that he should divorce my mother for being depressed. This woman had never so much as taken a single aspirin for a headache. It is so easy for someone to judge another person when he or she has never fought the same kind of battle.

Thousands of our service men are coming home from having served two and some as high as three tours of duty. They are severely depressed and suffering from PTSS. Can you just imagine one of them coming to our Lord Jesus and asking Him to heal them and Jesus telling them "a spirit of slap" is all over me! NO WAY!!!

Suicide takes the lives of nearly 30,000 Americans every year. Over half of all suicides occur in adult men, ages 25-65. Depression is the leading cause of suicide. The good news is that 80% of people that seek treatment for depression are treated successfully.

I am reminded of a time when one of the leading Christian women in our little home town of Richmond, Kentucky came to visit my dear mother while she was having one of her nervous breakdowns. She told my mother that she had so much to be thankful for: a beautiful home, a lovely family, a nice income, etc. In other words, she didn't have any reason to be depressed. With tears streaming down her cheeks, my mother humbly said, "I would give everything I own if I could just get well." Later when I was going through that same hell and was fighting thoughts of suicide, I regretted the way I had judged my mother so harshly, but you cannot put life in reverse. Thankfully, my mother forgave me, but I can tell you it was very hard for me to forgive myself.

I will not try to get into all of the clinical sides of manic-depressive types of mood disorders and their symptoms in my book. That is not the main focus or purpose I have written this book. Patty Duke wrote a wonderful book entitled, *A Brilliant Madness* that explains all of the different types of mood disorders and I highly recommend it if that is something that you would like to explore further. My main objective for writing is to tell you how I was healed so that you can receive an impartation of faith to believe for your healing for *God is no respecter of persons. (Acts 10:34)*

I am also writing this book to try to enlighten those of you who may know someone who is suffering from depression. Young or old, rich or poor, Christian or non-Christian, depression can strike anyone at anytime. You may be actually contributing to their demise and making them feel worse by saying or doing the wrong things that can create guilt or condemnation. I want to iv

give you some vital information that can help you to deal with someone you know who may be in the "black hole". You never know but what you may actually prevent someone from committing suicide.

I know that our family made my mother feel much worse by our insensitivity and ignorance. It is my hope that after you read my book that you will develop a greater degree of compassion and sensitivity to others who are around you who are suffering. One day you may be in their shoes.

I recently heard that 50 percent of all prescriptions are anti-depressants so I called our local drug store and spoke with the pharmacist. She said that she thought that more than 50 percent of the prescriptions were antidepressants. Our world has never been in such turmoil but I come to bring you good news! God is still on the throne and He cares for you. His word has never changed, *"He is the same yesterday, today and forever." (Hebrews 13:8)*

Another reason that I am writing a book is to give God all of the praise and the glory for my healing. God led me to use the doctors and antidepressants for over 17 years, and I thank God for their help. But the time came when the antidepressants were actually making me suicidal because they were working against me. My back was against the wall. When medical science has gone as far as it can go, and you have no one else to look to for your healing, look to Him; the Lord Jesus Christ. He still saves, heals and delivers us from sin, sickness and poverty no matter who we are, what we have done, or how bad the disease is!

Beloved, if you are depressed or know someone who is depressed and you have tried everything you know to get free, this book is for you. I have been there and done that for over 40 years and I can tell you from my own personal experiences that God does not condemn you for feeling this way. He is near the broken hearted. *[18]The LORD is nigh unto them that are of a broken heart; and saveth such as be of a contrite spirit. (Psalm 34:18) God did not send His only son into the world to condemn the world but through Him we might be saved and healed from all of our diseases. (John 3:17)* There is hope for you today, and while you may not receive an instantaneous healing, it is my prayer that God will give you a new revelation of His perfect will for your life. I pray that you will have the faith to stand on God's word and resolve never to give up until you receive the healing that Jesus Christ has already paid for.

Satan wants us in the pit or "the black hole" so that we will stop dreaming. His ultimate plan is to stop us from fulfilling God's dream for our lives.

Come now therefore, and let us slay him (Joseph), and cast him into some pit, and we will say, Some evil beast hath devoured him: <u>and we shall see what will become of his dreams.</u> (Genesis 37:20)

God's mandate to me is to bring inner healing to those of you who have a broken heart. The Bible calls depression, "the spirit of heaviness".

*To appoint unto them that mourn in Zion, to give unto them beauty for ashes, the oil of joy for mourning, the garment of praise for the **spirit of heaviness;** that they might be called trees of righteousness, the planting of the LORD, that he might be glorified. (Isaiah 61:3)*

The Spirit of the Lord is upon me, because he hath anointed me to preach the gospel to the poor; <u>he hath sent me to heal the brokenhearted, to preach deliverance to the captives, and recovering of sight to the blind, to set at liberty them that are bruised. (Luke 4:18)</u>

<u>A bruised reed shall he not break</u>, and the smoking flax shall he not quench: he shall bring forth judgment unto truth. (Isaiah 42:3)

Call unto me, and I will answer thee, and show thee great and mighty things, which thou knowest not.

(Jeremiah 33:3)

CHAPTER 1:

༄

A COLD WINTER DAY

It was going to be another long and bitterly cold winter day. Most all of Kentucky had been blanketed with a blizzard of snow a few days before, almost as though God had opened a giant bottle of white glitter and sprinkled it all over our little town of Richmond.

I lay in bed that morning – motionless-- as I heard my husband getting ready to go to work. David had a good job as a Customer Engineer for IBM which required him to do quite a bit of traveling in the neighboring rural towns. With his income, we were able to build a home on five beautiful rolling acres in the country. Our two sons were in elementary school at the time, and I was a stay-at-home mom. The boys were in heaven on this little piece on land, because they could spend hours playing in the nearby creek, catching snakes and tadpoles. In the spring time, our little Beagle mix, Duchess, would find rabbit holes with baby rabbits in them. There was always something exciting for the boys to do in the country.

The roads were icy this particular day, but there was school and it was time to get the boys up. They were usually pretty good about getting up and facing another day. I was always relieved when they were all out the door so that I could lie in bed all day without feeling guilty. I didn't sleep the whole time; I just had no energy to do anything mobile. I had no knowledge about being bipolar at that time. All that I knew was that I felt lazy, useless and miserably depressed most of the time. Just before the boys came home I would drag myself out of bed and put on my make-up and get dressed. I rarely did much housework or cooking because my energy level was so low.

One particular morning I thought if I had to stay at home alone all day and fight my demons, I would lose my mind. David was backing out of our long drive-way when all of a sudden, I jumped out of bed and ran out the front door waving my arms and yelling at the top of my lungs, "Come back, come back!" Luckily, he saw me and backed the truck up. I caught up with him and he rolled down the window. He had this look of great concern and compassion when he saw the look of desperation in my eyes. Tears were streaming down my cheeks. My hair was disheveled and I was wearing a paper thin summer nightgown standing there bare-footed. The icy wind was cutting me in two. Breathlessly I asked, "Can I just ride with you today and sit in the truck while you take your calls? Yes, sure you can." He said. We walked back into the house and I threw on some jeans, grabbed my coat and off we went. Seeing the countryside and having his company during the day was more pleasurable than lying in bed and feeling miserably lonely all day.

There were several more times that winter when I would ride with him again just to get out of the house. I especially enjoyed seeing the Christmas decorations in the country stores, which gave me a little Christmas spirit. I believe these trips kept me from falling into what I call, "the black hole"; a place where you reach complete and utter hopelessness and feel like you are in hell away from God. Doctors call this a catatonic condition where most people have to be hospitalized and have electric shock therapy to bring them out.

We lived in that house for two years and the entire time we lived there I was depressed. The depression had started right after the birth of our first child. Our neighbor said that it had been an Indian burial ground in the past and that perhaps that had something to do with it. If that were the case then why wasn't my husband and both of our sons depressed?

In retrospect, I realize I should have gone for medical help back then. I have no idea why I didn't unless it was fear that I would be hospitalized. David and I were pastors all that time and it was then that I began hiding behind a mask. I became so accustomed to wearing a mask at church and at home that I hardly realized I was even wearing it. I was able to attend the services and was very involved in ministry but there was always this cloud of darkness that seemed to hang over me.

A major conflict began with my faith and my God. I couldn't figure out why God wouldn't heal me if He really loved me and I didn't know who to go to for the answers.

Clint, Cheryl and Hunt Mother's Day 1991

Thus saith the LORD that made thee, and formed thee from the womb, which will help thee; Fear not, O Jacob, my servant; and thou, Jesurun, whom I have chosen.

(Isaiah 44:2)

CHAPTER 2:

❧

GROWING UP IN KENTUCKY

My parents were self-taught, successful residential and commercial building contractors in Lexington, Kentucky. We moved numerous times. The longest I ever lived in one house, prior to marriage, was five years. Toward the end of my junior year, the building business became very difficult for my father and he felt we needed to move where there was not so much competition. I was not happy about moving. I had several good friends in Lexington and a horse named "Rita" that I loved more than God. My parents never supported my love of horses. They were too afraid that I would get hurt and their pocketbooks could not support the luxury of owning a horse. When I was four, we lived in Louisville, Kentucky. My sister was eight years older than I and she took riding lessons. I must have fallen in love with them then because I can never remember not wanting one. I remember seeing a Shetland pony advertised in a catalog and asking my mother to buy it for me. She pretended to write and order one. Later she told me they had sold out of them.

Someone came by and took my picture age 5.

Later, when I was about eight or nine, we moved back to Lexington behind a horse farm which was being sold off as building lots. I remember the first time I went to check out the back yard and there were two big barns on about 50 acres surrounded by plank fencing. I saw some mares and foals out grazing on the famous "bluegrass". I went over and picked up some grass and reached through the fence, trying to coax a chestnut foal to eat out of my hand. The moment I ran my hand over its neck, I was hooked. It felt like velvet; so slick and shiny. The mom even came up and sniffed my hand and then she whinnied and called the foal away.

One day I walked up a steep hill and I went up to a barn located about a block away from our house. I remember not being afraid of anything and sauntered right up to one of the grooms working there. I asked him, "Mister, could you please tell me how much one of those horses cost?" He smiled real big and said, "Fifty cents." I said, "I have that much money in my piggy bank!" and ran home as fast as I could. I grabbed my little orange carnival piggy bank filled with coins and off I went back to the barn. I was sitting on the barn floor and began shaking out my coins; showing the grooms how much money I had. They were all smiling when all of a sudden my father came by and gave me a long talking to. He had no idea what he was in for down the road.

Later on, when I was in the fifth grade, we moved again. The first thing I noticed was that our house just so happened to be located behind a huge boarding stable. I could see there were lots of kids out riding in the snow and having a ball.

When I was born, my parents got a Beagle/Wirehaired terrier mix puppy they named "Tish". She would sleep under my bassinet and after I got older she followed me everywhere I went. I was a natural explorer and off Tish and I went to the barn to see what I could see.

Tish and me 1951

I was never shy. My sister told me that when I was very young I would go up and down our street knocking on doors and asking the neighbors if they had any children I could play with. Now I went to the barn to see if there were any kids my age that I could get to know so that I could ride their horses. Fortunately, I became acquainted with one really nice older girl named Janice who had a beautiful dapple gray gelding named "Frosty" and a chestnut gelding named "Copper". To those of you who may not know, a gelding is a male horse that has been castrated. I begged Janice to teach me how to ride, and to my surprise she agreed. She was one of the nicest people I have ever known and I will always be grateful to her for teaching me the basics of riding. I couldn't afford to pay her anything but agreed to clean her stalls and help groom her horses in exchange for lessons. The arrangement worked out perfectly for me and I think Janice enjoyed watching me develop my natural equestrian abilities. Soon I began asking for a horse of my own, but my father said that he could not afford one. Every night I prayed to God that He would give me a horse. I was obsessed with this dream. I believe it was my destiny.

I got to know some other girls at the barn. One day I remember going up there and seeing a girl standing there talking with her father. She had a big beautiful palomino that she hadn't ridden in a few months because she had her tonsils removed. It was bitter cold that day and she was afraid to ride him. I very confidently told them that I could ride him! I was sure that it would be alright. After much persuasion, her father reluctantly agreed. I had obviously convinced him that I was a good enough rider even as an 11 year old. The next thing I know, I was up on his back. We started to walk when suddenly he reared straight up. I fell off backwards onto the cold muddy ground. Luckily I was not hurt, but I didn't learn my lesson. I was always putting myself in harm's way by over mounting myself. I just had no fear of horses. I would never tell my parents if I got hurt for fear they wouldn't let me go back to the barn.

Then one day I met a young girl there whom I will call Mary to protect her name. Mary was adopted by an older couple. She had beautiful blond hair and blue eyes and was as cute as a button. But she was spoiled rotten by her doting older parents. Mary had won a Shetland pony named "Sonny Boy". He was sorrel in color with a flaxen mane and tail. Mary would jerk Sonny's bridle so hard that blood would poor from his mouth because of the hard steel bit. Then she would kick him in the stomach. I was horrified and began crying. I begged her not to hurt Sonny, but she did this repeatedly. She and I became good friends and eventually we began spending the night at each other's homes. Later Mary's father bought her a big, beautiful chestnut gelding that was a hunter jumper. I went out with Mary one afternoon and she tried to take him over a jump when he refused. All of a sudden she began jerking his bridle so hard that blood ran out of his mouth. I could tell she had broken off one of his teeth. I yelled at her and started to leave and I told her I was never going to talk to her again if she hurt him anymore. She begged me to stay and promised me she would stop. I remember thinking to myself that if I ever adopted a child, I would never spoil them. I couldn't stand cruelty to an animal.

We didn't live there but one year and then we moved again to a beautiful house on Williamsburg Road in Gardenside Estates. Back in the 60's, the area was close to beautiful horse farms that were still undeveloped. It was in this house where my whole life would change. I still kept in touch with the girls that I had made friends with at the barn and have many wonderful memories of those days. Later I became involved in 4-H Horse and Pony Clubs and rode whenever and wherever possible.

My beautiful mother, Lorene Bays Bolton.

Later, when I was 15, I went to a Catholic summer camp in Erlanger, Kentucky because they offered horseback riding. While I was there, I noticed the instructor was riding a beautiful chestnut American Saddlebred mare. I found out her name was "Rita." She was 15.1 hands (a hand is 4") and full of spirit. I would watch the instructor gallop her over the hills with another horse and rider. My heart absolutely melted. She was the epitome of everything I had ever imagined the perfect horse would be.

My handsome father, Charles Emmitt Bolton.

One day when I went to eat, I noticed there were some signs attached to the poles in the cafeteria that read, "FREE HORSE, INQUIRE WITHIN." I thought to myself, "Free horse; what in the world is this all about?" So I asked about the signs and I was told that you could take a horse home for the winter and then they would come and pick it up in the spring. That way you could get the privilege of riding the horse pretty much all fall and winter but, they would come and get the horse in time to be used again for camp season. Well, this got my attention real fast. I had to find out if Rita was one of the horses that you could take home. To my surprise, the answer was "Yes." I began to pray earnestly that my father would let me take her home.

My parents came to pick me up on a Friday. I had been there for five days. As soon my parents loaded up my bags and we got into the car, I began begging. The drive was a little over an hour and my poor father said, "I wish to goodness we had never let her come up here! She's gonna drive me crazy!" I could see him rubbing the back of his head as he did when he would get really agitated over something. I was relentless; without mercy. On and on the begging went until he threatened to ground me if I asked him one more time. I had to find a way where there was no way. My father said they simply could not afford to take care of a horse. In the meantime I had an idea. I could get three other girls to go in with me to share expenses and we would each take turns on different days riding her. It was a brilliant idea and I now believe in looking back that only the Lord put this together for me. Sure enough, I got the other girls to talk with their parents and we put it in writing. It worked! My father and mother both saw my determination and dedication and they decided to give me a chance. I was absolutely ecstatic. All summer long as I waited for the big day of arrival, I would sit at my desk and write "Rita" over and over just like an expectant mother does in trying to decide names for her baby. Or like when you have a boyfriend and you sit and write his name over and over.

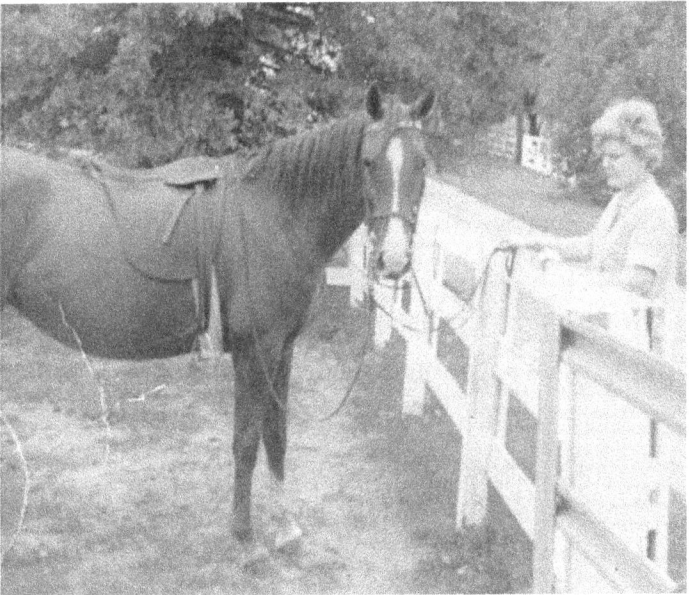

Rita and my Mother 1967

Then quite unexpectedly, one day I ran in the house and walked right past her saddle and bridle and didn't even notice it. Our house was a large ranch (one story) on a half acre corner lot in Lexington, Kentucky. My parents had their office at home in our garage and we had a screened porch connecting the garage to the house. The bridle and saddle were on a table in the porch. My father finally came up to me and asked, "Aren't you goin to go see your horse?" I looked at him puzzled. He said, "Right there is her saddle and bridle! She arrived this afternoon and she's at the barn." I quickly looked and saw her tack and ran over and picked it up. Immediately I headed for the barn. My dad said, "I'll drive you down there." My heart was pounding inside; I could not believe my dream was finally coming true! The moment I saw Rita, I just melted with love inside. God had finally answered my prayer. I spent every minute of my free time at the barn. I loved grooming and bathing her. I even loved cleaning her stall. I would sing to her and tell her all of my problems.

We boarded her about a mile from our house and I would walk down there every day after school. I would see Rita proudly standing there by the fence with her head way up high watching for me to come to her. I had very few riding lessons prior to her coming, but gained tremendous confidence riding her over the next few months. I loved galloping her up the hills bareback and soon got in tip top physical condition. Those days that I spent with my horse were some of the happiest days of my entire life.

Then the following spring, sometime toward the end of April, I came home one day from school and my mom showed me a post card laying on the dining room table that had come a few weeks prior. It was very brief, "We will be there to pick up Rita on April ___ and will be calling you on such and such a date to have you arrange to meet us." I looked at the date and they had come and picked up Rita earlier that morning. I went berserk! I started screaming and crying and was border line hysterical. I couldn't have been anymore heartsick if they had told me my parents were dead. I had just lost my best friend in the whole world. I felt I had nothing left to live for. My parents felt horrible for me, even though they never let on like they cared. They just kept telling me that they couldn't afford a horse.

By this time, I was almost 16 and could get a waitress job at Jerry's Restaurant, which was fairly near our home. I thought to myself, "If I can get a job, then they will let me get the horse." I had to be able to pay for Rita's board and all of her expenses.

Finally, after a season of time, my father decided he would sacrifice and buy me a horse. He tried to talk me into getting another horse but I had already bonded to Miss Rita. She had stolen my heart and I was molded to her sides. He agreed to buy her for my 16th birthday. I did my part in working and taking care of her and it was the best decision my parents ever made for my life. Not only was riding good exercise for me physically, but she was therapy for me mentally and emotionally.

Because they have no changes, therefore they fear not God.

(Psalm 55:19)

CHAPTER 3:

❧

THE ACCIDENT

The date was June 6th, 1968. I shall never forget that day. I had just finished my junior year at Lafayette High School and celebrated my 17th birthday on June 3rd. A boyfriend of mine wanted me to take him riding. One of my best girlfriends knew the owners of the famous Darby Dan horse farm and she got permission for us to ride there. She brought her horse and borrowed two others. Between the three of us, there were only two saddles and I chose to ride bareback. The horse I chose to ride was a retired race horse named Pax. "Suripax" was his registered name. He was a huge bay Thoroughbred that I had never ridden before and he stood 17 or 18 hands tall at the withers. He was trained to do competitive jumping but I had never jumped before. He was tacked up with a light snaffle bit bridle and no chin chain. If you don't know anything about horses, this was like wearing flip-flops to go ice skating. This bit has little control over a horse.

This famous stable was surrounded by white plank fencing with hundreds of acres of beautiful pastures. Springtime is one of my favorite times in Lexington because the bluegrass begins to green up and everything comes alive in nature. On this particular day, it was surreal as the robins were singing and the trees were laced with beautiful flower blossoms. The daffodils and buttercups lined the driveways all along the pastures. It was truly picturesque and the weather was perfect for our joy ride. As soon as I mounted I remember saying, "I have never been hurt before, so I'm not afraid now." My confidence was soaring. I made the remark, "I don't know why this horse has such a bad reputation; he seems so gentle!" I gently put my heel to his side and asked him to canter for me. He quickly followed my signal and it felt like riding a smooth rocking horse; so comfortable. I felt so safe and secure. We were having such a wonderful time.

We had not been riding but just a few minutes when all of a sudden, without any warning, Pax put his head down and lunged forward. He bolted into a dead run gallop, just like he had done hundreds of times on

the race track. Evidently when he saw my friends trying to catch up with me from behind, his training came
into play and he totally forgot that I was on his back. I
knew from the get-go that I was in serious and immediate danger. I dropped my reins, wrapped my arms
around his neck and began to scream at the top of my
lungs, ***"GOD, STOP HIM! STOP HIM GOD!"*** I could see
a barn ahead which was a quarter of a mile away with
only half of the door opened. If he darted into the barn
at such high speed, I would get my leg ripped off. If on
the other hand, he decided to jump the fence attached
to the barn, being bare back I would fall off. I could only
imagine breaking my neck or becoming paralyzed. I
was beyond terrified. After holding on with all of my
might for what seemed like hours, God unexpectedly
answered my prayer. Pax's back foot slid on the slick
road and immediately I fell over to my left side. I tried
to hold on to his mane with all of my strength, but in
a split second I hit the ground and rolled. Instantly my
legs went numb. My friends caught up with me and
wanted to know if I was ok. I tried to get up but my legs
wouldn't move. They thought I was faking it so one of
them rolled my leg over. Blood was running down the
road and gravel was embedded in my legs and ankle.
They knew they had to call for help.

It took the ambulance about 45 minutes to find me since we were at such a remote location. By the time we reached the hospital my hip was throbbing with unbearable pain. I lay there waiting for my parents to get to the hospital and sign a release form for the doctors. I had completely dislocated my left hip and torn every ligament and tendon around it. I thought I would die before the doctor finally gave me an enormous shot of pain killer that looked like the size of a small baby bottle. The doctor and nurses helped me to gently slide over to another table and let my leg and hip hang over to my left side. The doctor then took my leg and moved it forward and then backward in such a way that the joint popped back into place. I felt instant relief. I asked him if I could go home. He began to show me the x-rays and I saw my pelvis joints looked like two large butterfly wings. On the right side, there was clearly a ball in the socket. On the left side the ball joint of my hip was well below the socket. He told me that I would have been much better off to have broken my hip because I had torn every ligament and tendon in that area which would take at least one year for them to completely heal. The doctor told me that I could not ride horses until that healing took place. In the meantime I was sent home in a spica cast. I would have to use crutches until the last of August. It was like a death sentence. What in the world would I do now? My whole world centered around my horse and riding. All I ever thought about from the time I was four years old was horses. Now my world had fallen apart. One minute we were having the time of our lives, the next minute I was facing death right in the eyes. There is no doubt in my mind that God gave me Rita and there is no doubt that his angel caused Pax to slip so that I would not be permanently injured or even killed. But God had to permit horses to come off the throne. I didn't realize it at the time but He had a higher calling on my life. It was pruning time.

During this time when I was recuperating with my dislocated hip, my mother was suffering from one of her major depressions. She had been catatonic and was hospitalized and had to have shock therapy. Fortunately for me, she was now home but she was still not herself. Her energy level was still very low and she just wasn't interested in spending time with me. For the most part I was in bed alone but my friends did come by just about daily to spend awhile with me. My mother had a friend who had been a nurse and she would come up and check on me and bathe me, thank God.

I remember one particular morning that I wish I could forever forget. I was just learning to walk on crutches and had hobbled outside to the back yard. It was summertime and I was ready to get out of the house and enjoy the beautiful weather after the long harsh winter. My mother went out there and wanted to put her arms around me. She told me she loved me. When she reached out to put her arms around me, I jerked back and angrily spoke these words which I wish I could take back, "Don't touch me! You've waited 16 years too late!" God, I wish I had only understood where she was and what she was feeling back then but life has no reverse. I don't remember her trying to hug me again for a long time. She was too fragile to handle any more rejection. People who are suffering from depression feel very weak emotionally and they have a low self esteem. They have usually suffered from rejection and they need extra love and affirmation. NEVER and I mean NEVER SAY HURTFUL THINGS TO SOMEONE WHO IS SUFFERING FROM DEPRESSION. It is not the time to bring up something they said or did in the past to offend you. It is not the time to put them down by making unkind remarks. If I could go back to that one day, I would have hugged my dear mother and told her how much we loved her and missed her when she was gone to the hospital. No telling what that would have done for her. It is the little things we say that hurt and kill, but it is also the little things we say and do that can make a person feel like a million bucks. ***Death and life is in the power of the tongue.*** (Proverbs 18:21) It doesn't cost us anything to speak kind words, precious one and they are so priceless to someone who feels like they have nothing to live for. Our words are so powerful and they can help speed up a person's healing or they can keep a person down. This is probably one of the most important lessons that Jesus taught me personally and I am so happy I can share this lesson with you today because it is so important.

And we know that all things work together for good to them that love God, to them who are the called according to his purpose.

(Romans 8:28)

CHAPTER 4:

꧁

A NEW LOVE

Later on that summer, after I could go out on crutches, my parents began showing my brother and me around Richmond, Kentucky, a little city that they were planning to move us to about 30 miles away. My brother was four years younger than I was and he didn't seem to mind too much. He and my dad were best of friends and they always "did their thing" on the week-ends regardless of where we lived. It wouldn't really affect him that much because Dad was his best friend. But I felt alone, isolated and hostile about the entire move. I had no one to talk to about it. Dad made it clear that we were moving and it was not open for discussion. Case closed. Done deal. I was not close to either of my parents, especially my father. He was what --I thought at that time-- too strict. But now that

I am a parent, I don't think that he was too strict at all but he didn't balance his discipline with love or affection. When you discipline a child without love or having a relationship, you create anger and rebellion in that child. Coming from his dysfunctional childhood, he didn't have the tool bag to know how to show me love. He was an excellent provider and protector but he did not have the emotional capacity to express love to women. What I did notice was that he could readily show love to my brother and he taught him everything. From the time my brother was literally in diapers he began taking him fishing and hunting. Later he began teaching him all about building houses. He mentored my brother and knew how to connect with him in an intellectual and emotional way. With all of us women, he was crippled from his abusive step-mother and could not relate to us in a warm or affectionate way. I will tell more about that in another chapter. Getting back to this move, I was in pain. Not physical pain anymore, but emotional pain. When people are in emotional pain and distress they look for ways to escape. I had to sell Rita because of our move. This was another traumatic event but it had to be done. I sold her as a brood mare to a man in Danville.

Mom and Dad. So happy together.

With my pain, my only way of escape I thought was to get married. I began to look for a prospect. I was desperate. Not only did I want out of the house but I wanted and desperately needed someone to love me.

I was enrolled at Madison Central High School and I met a really nice girl named Donna and we became good friends. I invited her to spend the night with me. I was looking at her wallet photos and noticed a photo of this really cute boy drinking a bottle of beer in a sailor suit. I asked her who he was and she told me he was her brother. David was 20 years old and in the

Navy and stationed in Norfolk, Virginia. I asked if he was going with anyone and to my surprise her answer was, "No, he just broke up with someone." She told me she would try to set us up on a blind date whenever he got time off and came home on a visit. A few weeks went by and I had given up on him asking me. Then on January 3rd, 1969, I got a call at around 3:00 p.m. from another friend of mine who wanted to know if I would go out with David that night on a blind date with her and her boyfriend. I said, "Yes!" I was so excited that I began to primp three hours before our date. It was bitter cold and snowing but my heart felt warm and all aglow with feelings of anticipation. I had hope burning inside for the first time since we had moved to Richmond.

It was love at first sight for both of us. I know you hear this often said and most people will tell you that you are really feeling infatuation when you get that flaming, burning love and your heart beats really fast whenever you are with the one you love. But I do believe that it was genuinely more than just a physical attraction for both of us. We had a deep connection and wanted to be together all of the time.

David came home the following week-end and then later he came home on a ten day leave near the end of January. I made sure I was ready for him. I had a friend of mine make me a navy blue sailor suit. I was so tiny I couldn't find clothes to fit me. I was 5'10" and only weighed 129 lbs. Horseback riding had kept me in top physical shape and I didn't have an inch of fat on my body. When David picked me up I told him I had had my sailor suit made just for him. He was totally impressed and thrilled about my obvious love for him. He wrote me a letter and asked me what I thought about marrying him. We later discussed it and decided that if my parents wouldn't sign because I was only 17, that we would run off to Jellico, Tennessee where you could get married at 17. When I told my parents our plans, needless to say they were not happy, but my father knew that if he didn't sign, we would run away. So a week later, on January 29th, 1969 at 6:00 p.m., we tied the knot at a little Nazarene church. Our wedding was very simple and only about 50 people attended but God honored our marriage vows and covenant to Him. Little did either of us dream what God had in store for us.

David and Me, 1969

Jesus answered and said unto him, Verily, verily, I say unto thee, Except a man be born again, he cannot see the kingdom of God.

(John 3:3)

CHAPTER 5:

୬⧉୬

BORN AGAIN

Shortly after David got out of the Navy, I became pregnant with our first child. I was only 19 and David and I both were attending the First Baptist Church in Richmond, Kentucky. There was a revival during Easter season and the evangelist preached about the crucifixion of Christ. He went into great details. I had seen several movies on TV about Jesus' death and had been to Sunday School off and on all of my life and knew that Jesus died on the cross, but I had never heard specific details about his scourging and the unbelievable agony He suffered prior to the crucifixion. I had always thought that I was a Christian since I believed in Jesus, but the evangelist explained that you have to be born again (John 3:7) and invite Jesus Christ into your heart. This was far more than just having a head knowledge, or mental assent and having a passive faith. This was believing that a sinless God died for <u>my</u> sins and making Him the Lord of <u>my</u> life. That Sunday, my mother and I accepted Jesus Christ as our personal Lord and Savior. Someone said that all other gods want you to die for them but Jesus is the only God that died for us.

That following week, the pastor visited us and he asked David if he didn't want to give his heart to the Lord so that we could have a Christian family. David explained to the pastor that he thought that was just too easy. He was brought up in another denomination and was taught you had to come to the altar and cry tears of heartfelt repentance and beg God to save you. He thought you had to clean yourself up before Jesus would accept you. Our pastor showed David the scripture that read, *"Our righteousness is as filthy rags." (Isaiah 64:6)* In other words, we could not be saved by cleaning ourselves up. We are saved by the free gift of salvation. *"For God so loved the word, that He gave His only begotten Son, that <u>whosoever believeth in Him should not perish, but have everlasting life.</u> (John 3:16).* The pastor then read *"But what saith it? The word is nigh thee, even in thy mouth, and in thy heart: that is, the word of faith, which we preach; That <u>if thou shalt confess with thy mouth the Lord Jesus, and shalt believe in thine heart that God hath</u>*

raised him from the dead, thou shalt be saved. For with the heart man believeth unto righteousness; and with the mouth confession is made unto salvation." (Romans 10:8-10). We are saved by faith and grace, not by our works and we need to confess Jesus is Lord with our mouths in order to be saved. So after the pastor read David the scriptures the pastor asked David again if he wanted to be saved and David said, "Yes." Thank God for a pastor who cared enough to come to our home and who was courageous enough to ask David to pray with him.

Later David and I were baptized together in water. I was barely showing signs of pregnancy when I was baptized. I began to hunger after the Lord. I would kneel by my bed and say, "Lord if there is more show me." I was so hungry for miracles and the power of God.

Unto the woman he said, I will greatly multiply thy sorrow and thy conception; in sorrow thou shalt bring forth children; and thy desire shall be to thy husband, and he shall rule over thee.

(Genesis 3:16)

CHAPTER 6:

❦

POSTPARTUM DEPRESSION

I remember it well; the first time I felt depressed. I was 19 years old and had recently given birth to our first child, a beautiful healthy son. He was nearly two weeks late and weighed in at a whopping 9 lbs ½ oz. A few days later, I starting feeling depressed. I had unwanted thoughts that I would never speak about they were so horrible. My husband and I had prayed for me to become pregnant. It wasn't like we hadn't planned for this child, but I was having a horrible case of the postpartum blues. My mother had warned me that she had experienced this malady after childbirth but I had no idea that they would affect me so drastically. In my head I knew I wasn't in agreement with the thoughts I was experiencing but I couldn't control them. I felt so guilty. One day I vividly remember going to the bathroom and picking up a razor blade. At that moment, I wanted to slit my wrists and die. I began to cry out in desperation, *"God, if you will take away this depression and give me a reason for living, I will serve you all the days of my life!"* Nothing happened. I still felt depressed for several weeks afterwards. I didn't seek medical help but continued to pray. Eventually my health returned.

Our firstborn son, Clint. I was only 19 years old.

Then, four years later I gave birth to another beautiful healthy baby boy. I was determined not to have the postpartum blues with this child but mind over matter didn't prevent them from coming again. I couldn't believe that not only did I feel depressed but even worse than the first time. Day after day I prayed for the depression to leave and I begged God for strength to raise my two sons. Then I became extremely moody. Some days I would say horrible things to my precious husband and then later cry and ask him to forgive me. I didn't understand what was happening to my mind. My mood swings would range from euphoric to suicidal. I even threatened to divorce my husband at times and then would cry out to God to forgive me for acting like a pathetic Christian.

I remember witnessing to our neighbors and then something would happen and I would blow up and would curse so loud I knew they could hear me. I felt like such a hypocrite. I remember thinking that I wasn't going to witness to anyone anymore and I told my mom that I couldn't serve the Lord because I was such a rotten Christian. She told me, "It's better to stumble into heaven than to walk into hell." But the guilt and shame was beginning to overtake me. Thank God for a patient and loving husband.

I knew that my mother and grandmother had both suffered from severe, debilitating depression most of their lives. Neither my father, nor any of our immediate family members were patient and kind to Mother when she felt sad. We chided her for feeling sorry for herself. After all, we had a beautiful home and all the material things money could buy; she didn't have an excuse to feel depressed. Both my mother and grandmother were hospitalized on several occasions because they had become catatonic and could no longer function. The thought of having to undergo electroconvulsive therapy (ECT) as they had, terrified me. I knew if I didn't improve soon, I would have to go down that road.

A few years ago, Tom Cruise openly slammed his friend, Brooke Shields for taking Paxil while suffering from postpartum blues. He claimed that all she needed was vitamins. Cruise is a staunch member of the Church of Scientology. The general public rose up in anger against his judgmental and condemnatory comments and he later apologized. Shields has written a book about her ordeal. Post partum blues usually starts about three to four days after having a baby and can last several days or much longer. Let me just say right here that anytime anyone tells you that you should not go to a doctor or use medication for any health issue, regardless if it is postpartum blues, depression or an ingrown toenail, run! No where in the Bible does Jesus say that we are not to use physicians.

If you are suffering longer than a few days from post-partum depression, you need to consult your doctor as this can lead to severe clinical depression. You may need some mild antidepressants on a short term basis. Ignoring this type of depression is very serious as some women have been know to have complete nervous breakdowns from post-partum depression. Looking back I realize I suffered needlessly from this condition, but I never realized that I could get help for it.

There may be some holistic alternatives available which you can research on the internet. Regardless, don't suffer needlessly. Get help!

[11]*And he gave some, apostles; and some, prophets; and some, evangelists; and some, pastors and teachers.*

(Ephesians 4:11)

CHAPTER 7:

THE CALL

Soon after David and I got saved, I began watching the 700 Club and learned about the baptism in the Holy Spirit. I had never heard of the baptism in the Holy Spirit but continued seeking God for more of Him. I found out that there was a new little Assembly of God church being started in our town that believed in the gifts of the Holy Spirit and I went to visit. The church was being started in the back of an old dilapidated hospital in the emergency room.

When I first walked in the door, I remember seeing only a handful of people and they were praying at the altar. I noticed that the pastor, Rev. Dan Estes, was very young, about my age of 25 at the time. My thoughts were, "He is too young to teach me anything." I was going to quietly leave, hoping he had not heard me come in, but he quickly jumped up and ran over to greet me. His wife, Sharon, played the piano and then they asked everyone (there were only a few) to sit in a circle and Dan asked us if we had a testimony. I had never in my life heard people talk out loud in church before and I had never heard anyone give a testimony. I really enjoyed it. Then, Dan led us in a chorus, Halleujah, Halleujah. Not the famous Halleujah chorus but the little simple version. All of a sudden I felt the presence of the Holy Spirit. I had never felt this presence before in my life. At least if I had, I had not recognized it. I was so excited!

Then a few weeks later, a lady gave a message in tongues, which I heard for the first time. Some call this the language of angels or supernatural language. I really felt the presence of God then! I came home and told David that I knew this was God. No man could have made up that language and I felt the presence of God when she gave the message in tongues. Afterwards there was an interpretation. David was from a denomination that believed that tongues were of the devil and if you spoke in tongues you needed to find another church. Needless to say, he wasn't very excited when I reported what I had witnessed to him. But, the undeniable facts were that the more I attended this little charismatic church, the hungrier I became for more of the Lord. I began fasting and praying on a regular basis.

Pastor Dan preached about the baptism of the Holy Spirit and I began praying for the experience. "Seek the Lord, not tongues", the pastor told me. It seemed like everywhere I turned I was hearing a message about the baptism in the Holy Spirit. Even Pat Robertson was teaching about this amazing free gift. So, one day I wrote 700 Club and asked for the pamphlet about how to receive the baptism. I was so excited when it arrived. I remember putting my baby down for a nap and going into our bedroom and kneeling by our bed. I began to pray and ask God to fill me with His Spirit. I didn't feel anything. I re-read the pamphlet over and over. The Bible says, *"Or what man is there of you, whom if his son ask bread, will he give him a stone?" (Matthew 7:9)* Over and over I began reading all of the scriptures that proved that the baptism of the Holy Spirit is for whosoever will. Not just for a few chosen. So, I opened my mouth by faith and in my mind I heard a word. I spoke it out and then repeated it again and again. All of a sudden I felt the presence of the Lord so strong that I knew I had received.

After that experience, I would pray in English and then pray in tongues. At first I only had one or two syllables but as time went on I could hear more and more syllables. It takes faith to pray in tongues because you don't know what you are saying but *Jude 1:20 says beloved, <u>building up yourselves on your most holy faith, praying in the Holy Ghost.</u>* This is very important to remember for you to receive your healing. We will talk more about this in another chapter.

As time went on, I began to ask God to use me in a message in tongues and the interpretation. David and I used to meet with his cousin who was called to preach and we would have prayer meetings in our home. It was there that I began to try my wings and in other small groups. Finally I got up the nerve to step out in a church service. The more God used me, the more I wanted to be used. David was taking notice.

Soon David felt that God was calling him to preach. The ultimate confirmation came when the pastor asked him to preach. Before long Pastor Dan encouraged us to step out and began to pastor. Neither of us felt we were ready but we had such a burden to win souls that we had enough faith to step out. I remember how many times we were reminded of our youth by the members of the first church we pastored. David asked me to teach an adult Sunday School class and one of the ladies made the comment to David that she didn't think I could teach her anything since I was so young. Just like I had felt about Pastor Dan when we first started attending his church.

I had no idea that one of the ladies and her husband had not spoken to their son-in-law for three years and it just so happened that I began teaching on the "love" chapter, I Corinthians 13. I can tell you that it was very uncomfortable putting them together.

One time we had a fellowship dinner and the kitchen was so small that I had placed a bowl of beans over the top of one of the other lady's dish of macaroni and cheese. This lady let me have it. She told me that she didn't bring that dish to end up taking it home again. I quickly grabbed her macaroni and cheese and went around trying to make sure everyone took some. I was such a people pleaser. I cried all the way home after every service for months. I felt so inadequate to be a pastor's wife and to have the people tell me that I was inadequate was all that it took to push me over the edge. I had not even been raised in a Christian home and only occasionally went to Sunday School. I never observed a pastor's wife until we met Pastor Dan and

Sharon and I was nothing like Sharon. I felt like a fish out of water. Depression and anxiety began to set in on a regular basis.

David and I continued to serve as pastors and we ended up serving some rather large congregations. I remember feeling like I wanted to run away from church altogether but knew I couldn't. I felt totally trapped. God had called David to preach and *the gifts and calling of God are without repentance (Romans 11:29).*

I was good at hiding behind a mask both at home and in church. I never went to seek medical help because I kept listening to preachers who kept saying that all I needed to do was to confess that I had my healing and I would be healed. I just kept praying and believing for a miracle. I knew God could heal me and I had the faith. I would not go to the doctors. I don't know why I had such a fear of the doctors unless I was afraid they would put me in the hospital like my mother and grandmother. I felt condemned all of the time because I was depressed. I felt it was my fault because I didn't have enough faith. But God had a different plan. We just didn't know it yet.

And we know that all things work together for good to them that love God, to them who are the called according to his purpose.

(Romans 8:28)

CHAPTER 8:

⚜

GOOD NEWS

In 1984, I went to my OB/GYN for a routine exam and the doctor asked me if I had been lifting weights. I said "No, but the other day I carried my nine year old son up some steps to bed because he was so sick." I asked "Why?" The doctor said that I had a prolapsed uterus and he recommended that I have partial-hysterectomy and remove my uterus. I was only 33 years old. I was devastated at this news because I wanted a daughter more than life itself. Every time I saw a baby girl I just yearned for one of my own.

Also, I had made a vow to myself that I would die before I would have a hysterectomy because my dad had always said that my mother didn't have her nervous breakdowns until she had her hysterectomy. I just wouldn't consider it. But one day as I was in prayer, I heard that small still voice say, *"I want you to have the surgery and I want you to trust me."* I knew that I knew God had spoken to me. That's how it is when you are a Christian. If you walk with the Lord long enough, you will learn to "hear" His voice in your inner self. You will get it settled in your spirit and once you get it settled you will have a peace. There may be things you won't understand but your spirit will still have that quiet peace. When the devil speaks you will have no peace. He brings confusion and turmoil wherever he goes. So, I heard the voice of God and so it had to be. In my mind, I built my own little altar where I crucified my dream to have a daughter, but I never stopped wanting one. I look back now and again I can see how God was protecting me. Every time I had a baby, I sunk deep into depression. It seemed to trigger my bipolar condition worse and worse. But at the time I didn't know I was bipolar. I just had to trust in God.

Several years went by, and we were pioneering a church in Lexington, Kentucky. By this time, I was 40 and David was 43. I was working at the University of Kentucky in the International Affairs office. There began to be tremendous exposure on TV about all of the thousands of babies in orphanages in Romania because the dictator, Nicolae Ceusecu had forbidden any birth control. I would see the babies rocking back and forth in their cribs and weep uncontrollably. "Lord", I prayed, "Can we just have one of those little babies? We have four bedrooms and food enough to spare. Please, Lord, please let us adopt one of those babies." I began to beg David relentlessly. Finally, on one beautiful November afternoon, David and I went out to lunch together and he told me that he wanted me to check into adoption and that he would "consider" it. Now I knew that meant that more than likely David was going along with my desire. Later on I asked him why he changed his mind and he told me it was because he finally realized that I was never going to be happy if I didn't get a baby girl. It reminded me of my parents finally agreeing to buy me a horse because they realized I would never be happy if I didn't get one.

Immediately, I began calling around asking how to go about adopting a baby. I found out that it was not going to be easy. It would cost thousands of dollars to adopt from Romania and would require greasing everyone's palms from the US to Romania and you would have to stay there for weeks at a time. When I turned to other adoption agencies I found the news was just as discouraging. It seemed that only rich people could adopt. Priority was given to people who had no children.

To want a newborn baby girl was considered wanting a "blue ribbon baby" and they were as rare as hen's teeth. We were told we could not be sex specific because we already had two biological children and we would have to take an older child or a baby with some mental or physical handicaps.

There were days when people would put all kinds of fears on us about adopting. I hate to say this, but my dear mother was probably the worst. She was so afraid we were going to get a sick baby that would break us up financially with medical bills. And then there were all these naysayers who had to tell us about adopted kids who killed their parents or who rejected them after they found their biological parents. It was so bad that I remember praying desperately for God to confirm that it was His absolute perfect will and not my will. I told Him I didn't want to bring harm and hardship on our family and that if He couldn't send us a healthy baby that would adopt us in their hearts, then take away the desire and never grant my request. I had surrendered the desire of my heart.

Finally after months of inner turmoil, David and I met at the church with some men from the Full Gospel Business Mens' Association and I asked them to pray for me to get this settled. As they laid their hands on me, I had an open vision. I saw a girl about to give birth in a hospital bed. I knew she was going to have a C-section. I saw Jesus tell the birth mother that she couldn't keep the baby, that she carried the baby for someone else. I looked at the birth mother's face to see if she was going to want to take the baby back but she had a beautiful serene smile on her face as she was watching our family hold the baby. I laid the baby girl on my lap and I carefully examined her from head to toe and she was perfect in every way. Then, I saw our sons looking at her. My eldest son first picked her up and then held her for a while. Then, our youngest spoke up and said, "You've held her for long enough, let me hold her!" Then he held her for a while and all the while David was looking down at her and smiling from ear to ear. I knew, that I knew, from that day on that God was going to give us a "blue ribbon baby" and that she was His gift to our family.

Later on, David contacted a personal friend he knew from Brazil who was heavily involved in orphanages. He assured us that he would help us to find a baby girl. After a few weeks he called to say he had found a young mother who was expecting a baby girl and she was going to give her to us. She could not afford to care for her. We began sending over money to help her with medical expenses. The day came when she was due. We were ecstatic. The baby was born fine and healthy and we sent the birth mother the name to go on the birth certificate. We were waiting to get our home study done and all the paperwork completed for the visas, etc. We finally had everything completed after weeks of preparation. We had our airline tickets and our bags were *packed*. I had two weeks of vacation from work scheduled. We even had our nursery set up and a little basket lined with soft material to carry the baby in. David called our contact to find out exact details of where to meet him in Brazil. We were so excited we just couldn't wait to get there. Then, the unthinkable happened. I heard David say, *"She did? Oh, no!"* I looked at David's face and could see he had a look of great concern. I asked, "What happened?" David said, "She decided to keep the baby." I began to scream and cry so hard and so loud that our contact heard me and he asked, "Is that Sister Cheryl? Oh, no..Please tell her I will find her another baby."

I was crying so loud that I ran into my closet and sat on the floor so that David wouldn't hear me. I began wailing and rocking back and forth like the little inconsolable babies I had witnessed on TV. I felt like every bone, muscle and cell in my body had been beaten with a ball bat. How had I missed God on this? I felt so strongly that I had confirmation after confirmation that we were on the right track and now this? What was going on? All I could do was sob.

In a few minutes I called the airlines to see if we could get our money back. Of course, they said no. As God would have it, the lady at the airline ticket office asked me what happened. When I told her, she told me to watch the movie, *Immediate Family*. I asked her why? She told me that this young girl would change her mind; just wait and see because she would realize it would be best for her child in the end. This gave me a rope of hope to hold onto. That is just like the Lord. He won't allow us to be tempted above what we are able to bear. (1 Cor. 10:13). I felt so much hope after talking with her.

Then that very evening, a board member of a large church in Florida called David and invited him to come and try out to be their pastor that following Friday evening. On the way down to the church, I heard the voice of the Lord say, *"I want you to share what happened to you with the people. There is someone there who is going to help you get a baby."* When David preached that Friday evening, I went on the platform and shared what had happened to us regarding the adoption. As soon as the service was over, I wondered if there would be someone who would come up to me like I thought God had told me. Sure enough, as we went over to the Fellowship Hall following the service, a lady came up to me and her exact words were, *"I think I can help you get a baby."* Then she began telling me about a home nearby that helped young girls who were pregnant and often times they gave up their babies for adoption.

I contacted the director of the home and she told me that God had a child of promise for us; not to lose hope. My hopes were soaring again. We completed all of the paperwork for the third time and began to wait and pray. Then the morning of my birthday, on June 3, 1992, when I awoke I heard

How lovely on the mountains are the feet of them
*Who bring **Good News, Good News***
Announcing peace proclaiming news of happiness
Our God reigns, Our God reigns.

This comes from Isaiah 52:7

[7]*How beautiful upon the mountains are the feet of him that bringeth good tidings, that publisheth peace; that bringeth good tidings of good, that publisheth salvation; that saith unto Zion, Thy God reigneth.*

I told David that we were going to get good news that day because every time God gave me that chorus, I always received good news. Then a little later that morning, the director called us and she told us there was a young girl who wanted to meet us who was expecting a baby girl. She was unable to keep the baby and had already decided to place her baby girl up for adoption. I was beyond ecstatic! There was the good news!

I had been reading Ann Kiemel's book, *Open Adoption: My Story of Love and Laughter,* which gave me some great ideas about what to do before I met the birth mother. So in preparation for our big meeting, I gathered some photo albums to show her all about our family.

When I first locked eyes with "Sally", I knew she was the one even though we had not yet been formally introduced as of yet. I immediately felt a kindred spirit with her. She was young and quiet and had a beautiful face and spirit about her that made David and I both fall instantly in love with her. I knew by this time, that I could not allow my hopes to soar. I would not "go there" until the baby was ours.

Later on, Sally wanted me to go with her to the doctor to have an ultra sound and I got to see the baby moving all around. I wanted to adopt the birth mother too, she was so precious. Finally, on August 21, 1992, the director called us and told us our daughter had been born two days before. The birth mother had been very sick and had a c-section just as God had shown me. We were to come and see her but first we needed to sign the adoption papers at the attorney's office. After we finished, the attorney asked if we wanted to take the baby home. We were shocked and surprised but of course responded immediately, "Yes, can we?" and she said "Yes! Go and get your baby but you first have to get a car seat." David and I ran to Wal-mart and started throwing in everything we could think of we needed into the cart and off to the hospital we went.

I will never forget standing there pacing with excitement in the foyer of the hospital waiting for the nurse to call us in the room to see our precious baby girl. Behind us were all of the disappointments and failed plans to adopt in Romania, then the heartbreak over the failed adoption in Brazil and now, at long last, my faith was going to become sight.

Finally, what seemed like an eternity, they called us into a hospital room and wheeled in what I thought was the most beautiful, blue eyed, blonde haired baby girl I had ever seen in my life. I couldn't believe my eyes. She was awake and looking at us! She was so alert and sucking on her fingers. David and I were crying we were so overjoyed and couldn't wait to take her home just to love on her.

Megan when she was a few days old.

That was 18 years ago and I can tell you that she has been the absolute joy of our family and everything that God promised us she would be and much more.

And, behold, there was a woman which had a spirit of infirmity eighteen years, and was bowed together, and could in no wise lift up herself.

(Luke 13:11)

CHAPTER 9:

❧

DIAGNOSIS: BIPOLAR TWO

Right after David and I made our move to Florida, we were involved in a horrible car accident. We were having a revival with the late Evangelist Dr. Jerry B Walker. We had taken him out to dinner and were taking him back to his motel when all of a sudden an older large bodied vehicle started coming toward us head on. Before David could manage to get out of harm's way, the drunk driver slammed into us broadside. I had just removed my seatbelt and had been facing Dr. Walker who was seated in the back. I distinctly recall saying, "God will protect me, I don't need a seatbelt; we are all ministers." This was a statement I later came to regret. It was an act of presumption and the Bible says that we are not to tempt the Lord. (Matthew 4:7)

When the driver hit, I slammed into the windshield at an angle which struck my head on the side. David got the wind knocked out of him and he was having a hard time breathing. I fell on the floor and was addled and couldn't speak for a few minutes. We were taken to the hospital where I learned I had suffered a mild concussion and we both had some nasty bruises. Dr. Walker lost the feelings permanently in one of his legs from the seatbelt injury.

I didn't realize how much this head injury affected me at the time of the accident, but later on I began to suffer horrible panic attacks and depression. I was never the same after this blow to my head. I later learned that this is more common than most people realize. My chiropractor told me that his sister had been an actress on stage and after she had a head injury, she could no longer act.

Shortly after the adoption, I began to feel severely depressed. I was so depressed that I knew I had to seek medical attention. I knew I had everything a person could hope for in this life, just as my poor mother had: a wonderful loving husband, two wonderful healthy sons, a beautiful healthy daughter, a beautiful new home, a stable job. Why was I so depressed? Every time I went to church I wanted to run and hide. My energy level was so low I could hardly care for my precious baby. I would lie on the floor and play with her and sleep beside her. Inside I was fighting a war for my sanity. I kept fighting back thoughts of suicide. I had to hide behind a mask every time I went to church.

David and I were talking about how debilitating bipolar disorder is. It strips you of your dignity and self respect and all of your hopes and dreams. I told him that this disease reminds me of the poor bull in the bull fights in Spain. It has all of this enormous strength, beauty and power. The crowds cheer with a loud shout as the Matador comes into the ring! The Matador looks so small in statute compared to the enormous size and strength of the bull, but he has been in training for years to learn how to outwit and kill the bull with a simple strategy: he antagonizes the bull with his fiery red cloak in order to provoke him into charging. As the bull makes his charge, instantly the Matador plunges a razor sharp dagger into his shoulder muscle where the pain will be felt the most. Time and time again, the bull, unaware of the Matador's clever scheme to kill him, continues to charge headlong into the red cape. Little by little, the Matador wears down the strength of the bull; the blood is drained one dart at a time, sapping him of every drop of his powerful strength. His muscles are wracked in pain and he has no more will to fight. Even while the bull is down for the last time, the cruel Matador will jeer and wave the cape in front of him to prove to the crowds and to the bull that he has won the battle.

That is how it feels to live with bipolar disease. One day you are up and full of energy and have enormous creativity flowing through your veins. You want to paint, you want to sing, and you want to write or do whatever your gifts and talents are. You want to see people and go out and travel or go shopping. You draw others around you because of your joy and laughter that bubbles out of your inner most being. You bring life to everyone who comes near you. You are the life of the party. Ideas burst into your brain like the sun after a long hard winter. Then, out of no where, you feel a little less energetic than you did the day before. You are not rendered helpless, but you just feel like one of your carburetors is missing. Then the next day, you feel a little less energetic and it lasts a little longer. You don't feel like getting out of bed until noon. The next day you feel like every ounce of your blood has been drained from your body and you don't have the energy to get dressed. You barely have the energy to go to the bathroom. Nothing, absolutely nothing means anything to you. You have no desire to do anything. You feel worthless and absolutely helpless.

You feel so guilty because you are not contributing to the advancement of your household. You only want to close the blinds and sleep. Your only hope is that when you wake up you will feel some strength again. You can only go on living with the hope that the sun will shine again. Like the poor pathetic, helpless bull, the devil whispers in your ears, "Why don't you just kill yourself and get out of this pain? You know your family would be so much better off. You are worthless, you're a nobody, you don't take care of your family, you don't cook and you don't even like sex. What are you living for?" If it was not for the prayers of those around me, I know I would have taken my life by now.

David finally consulted a Christian psychiatrist from Emerge Ministries who had come to minister at our church. Dr. Richard Dobbins is the founder of Emerge Ministries in Akron, Ohio. He told us that his wife also had horrible post partum blues and the doctors blamed her depression on her faith. The faith preachers blamed her depression on the doctors. There has always been a division in the body of Christ; it seems, regarding faith verses medical science. Especially when it comes to depression. Many a person could have been saved if they had only gotten medical treatment but they were praying for divine healing and died. When my sister was about 12, she came down with pneumonia was dying. My mother told me that the physicians told my parents they had just come out with a drug that was their last hope to save her life. That drug was penicillin. As soon as they gave it to her, she began to recover. Don't ever tell me that God doesn't use the doctors and medical science to heal people. Back during the Civil War, thousands of soldiers died from common diseases that we now have gotten totally under control such as measles, mumps and diphtheria. There are different methods God has used in the Bible to bring about healing.

For the first time in my life my psychiatrist diagnosed me with bipolar II disorder. David and I were both shocked! We learned that there are many different types of bipolar or manic depressive disorders. The doctor prescribed prozac. I began to gain weight but felt better, though not completely up to par. I think the car accident was still a contributing factor.

My husband began to come under attack from some of the board members and their wives. They were complaining about having a pastor's wife who was depressed. Time and time again people would come up to me and say, "You don't look sick." It was because I was hiding behind a mask. In reality I was like the bull.

One of the board members said that he couldn't understand how anyone could feel like committing suicide. It was not only what he said, but how he said it. It was as if I was on a big time pity party, trying to sabotage the church name. Fortunately, he contacted us and apologized repeatedly and we have long since forgiven him. Most did not apologize. Some of the board members were not only condemning me for being depressed, but judging David and me as though it was our fault. One board member said, "How can you have a healing service when your own wife is sick?" On and on the accusations came.

I could feel the tension when I went to church. I knew there were those who were judging me without a shred of mercy. I could totally identify with Christ when the religious Pharisees falsely accused and mocked Him. This group was already gathering their wheel barrel of stones to throw.

I must point out that this was a church of about a thousand people. We saw hundreds of souls saved on a regular basis. My husband said that on the one hand he was having the greatest success of his ministry. On the other hand never was he under such attack.

When I learned how our people felt about me, it pushed me over the edge. On the one hand, I wanted to kill myself and get out of my pain; on the other hand, I wanted to raise my children and stay with my wonderful husband. I remember thinking, "Lord, if I could just go someplace where could I see some mountains and deer and quiet streams and just rest and get away from it all."

One day out of desperation, I called a suicide hotline and the lady at the other end asked me if I could go to a treatment facility called "Healing For The Nations" (www.healingforthenations.org) which was at that time located in Colorado and called Rapha Retreat Center. I told her that we didn't have the finances. Then she asked me if I could go to a retreat center in Colorado Springs where I could get some help. I told her "No" again because of the money. Then she said for David to ask the board and see if they would pay for my airline ticket if Rapha would provide a scholarship. I was desperate and brought the matter to David. Thankfully, the board agreed to pay for my airfare and I received a scholarship. The board wanted me to get fixed; the sooner the better. I could feel David even pressuring me to get "fixed". His job was on the line.

As soon as I got there, the first thing I noticed was the beautiful mountains. You could see Pike's Peak in the distance and there was a little creek on the property. In the early morning, there were wild sheep grazing in the grass right in front of the cabin and a gorgeous old castle that was at the top of a hill. Everything was exactly as I had wished for in my heart and more. God is so good.

At the retreat, I learned many things about myself which would take another book to write. There were two other pastors who were there and both of them had come because they were suffering from major depression. One had been hospitalized because he had become catatonic. There was one pastor from a large congregation in California who admitted he had been a hyper faith preacher and he had preached against taking medications for years. Now he had become depressed and had to take antidepressants. He was so torn because if he told his church members and the board about it, he was afraid he would be voted out. He said he had trained his church to be condemnatory toward others who were sick. He felt like a complete hypocrite. When I told about my own battle with depression and how I got on medication they both told me that it helped them.

I strongly recommend Healing For The Nations retreat center for anyone who is suffering from a low self-worth or any major issues in life where you feel stuck. I learned what a people pleaser I was and how I was believing lies about God and who He is. Healing For The Nations is now located in Georgia and is still carried on by Steve and Rujon Morrison. Their main focus is teaching about the lies and false beliefs that we tell ourselves about God, but their teaching goes much deeper in getting the truth of God's word from your head to your heart. The thing that I took away from this retreat is that my significance had to come from Christ and not from my husband, my children, my church or any other thing in life. My value is based upon what Christ paid for me, not what I do for Christ nor how popular I am with people. People will come and go, jobs will change, and everything changes around us sooner or later. There is nothing that we can count on that remains the same except the love of Christ. His love is unconditional and He will never leave nor forsake us.

When I left Colorado Springs, I began to ask God if I could just "be" and not "do" anything for Him in church anymore. I was so beaten down I didn't know who I was anymore but I knew that I was tired of being a people pleaser. I was tired of hiding behind a mask.

There hath no temptation taken you but such as is common to man: but God is faithful, who will not suffer you to be tempted above that ye are able; but will with the temptation also make a way to escape, that ye may be able to bear it.

(1 Corinthians 10:13)

CHAPTER 10:

❧

A WAY OF ESCAPE

David realized that he had to make some drastic changes in our lives if I was ever going to be whole again. My doctor told him that he needed to resign the church in order to get me out of the pressure cooker. It was not going to be easy to leave but we knew it was time to put my health first. Many would argue that we should have put the church first, regardless of how much it caused me to suffer. I just want to remind those of you who feel this way that Jesus said: *Husbands, love your wives, even as Christ also loved the church, and gave himself for it. (Ephesians 5:24)* If my husband had refused to leave the church, I most likely would have become catatonic or committed suicide. The Bible says *How think ye? if a man have an hundred sheep, and one of them be gone astray, doth he not leave the ninety and nine, and goeth into the mountains, and seeketh that which is gone astray? (Matthew 18:12)*

There are so many pastors' wives who feel so isolated, neglected and even abused by their husbands. Some feel like everyone else's problems are important to their husband but theirs. I believe that is because some pastors' total identities are in the success they feel they have as being a pastor, rather than who they are in Christ. Others love their ministries more than they love their families and totally neglect their own family.

Recently I heard a very prominent woman preach about her early days in ministry and how she had ministered more out of her own need to have an identity and to feel important rather than the needs of others. Later her heart totally changed and came into proper alignment with God's perspective.

I don't care how high upon the pedestal a minister is, he or she is never too holy or strong for the devil to overcome them with pride and lust. In fact, the more God uses you I believe the more the trials and temptations will come. Recently, a world famous healing evangelist openly admitted that he had contributed to the break up of his marriage by putting his ministry above his family. Everyone was shocked when the news broke but I had seen it coming for years. I told my husband that I was certain that his wife had to feel like a "preacher's widow" because of his schedule.

It is very hard to balance ministry with family but God created the family before he formed the institution of the church. On the flip side of that coin, God wants to be first over our family. We cannot excuse ourselves from serving Him because of our mate or our children, etc. Anytime we put anyone or anything before Christ, we are making them our idols and committing a sin.

Case in point: My father's father, my grandfather Doug, was such a man. Doug was saved in jail and when he came out he felt the call of God on his life to start preaching. He began to plant churches in eastern Kentucky and was very well loved by members in his congregation. Doug's wife, my grandmother, named May, died at the young age of 37. My Aunt Maderis told me that my grandfather was gone all of the time doing the work of the Lord. He left my poor grandmother home with five children to raise between the ages of newborn and 17. May had several miscarriages. They were "dirt" poor or as my aunt said, "Poor as a church mouse." When my grandmother died, my grandfather shortly remarried a widow named Nan, who had a young son,

Austin. Nan told my aunts that she didn't know why she married a man with "youngins", she hated "youngins".

My father was only 18 months old when his mother died and was still in diapers when his father remarried Nan. My father told me that Nan sadistically abused him on a routine basis. Yet on Sunday morning, she would get all dressed up, put on her hat and go to church. Nan would lock my father up in the closet for days and then hold a butcher knife at his throat and dare him to tell his father. My father was the youngest of all five children. Nan would call him names and belittle him constantly. My father was dark skinned and she called him, "Nig". Nan would make my father and his brother stay out in the cold garage all day long because she didn't want them to make a mess in the house. She told his older sisters to get out and they married as soon as they could at very young ages.

From left to right: Doug, my grandmother May Shelby
Bolton holding my father, Charles and Maderis. This photo
was the last taken of my grandmother before she passed
away at age 37. Circa 1922.

My father said that one time Nan locked him and his
brother out in the snow and the neighbors saw them
hovering against the chimney, trying to stay warm. The

neighbors told Doug that my father and his brother were going to freeze to death if he didn't make Nan let them come inside. I heard story after story about Nan's abuse but she made sure her son, Austin, was always cared for. He was younger than my dad. She would buy Austin toys and dare my father or his brother to touch them.

Let me tell you what happened. My father ended up dropping out of school at the age of 15 and getting a job at the tipple in the coal mines. Then he moved in with his sister, Maderis, who by that time had gotten married. Maderis was six years older than he was. At the age of 17, he and my mother met at the local drugstore. She always lit up when she would tell me about how they met. When my dad came in the drugstore, he spotted my mother and asked someone who she was. She was sitting with my father's cousin, Grant, and she asked him who that good looking boy was.

My mother was fair skinned and had red hair. My father was very dark skinned and had dark brown wavy hair. They made a handsome couple. They began dating right away. My mother said the moment she laid eyes on my dad she fell instantly in love with him and it was the same for him. He had to ride a bicycle or hitch a ride from someone to go see her.

My father later joined the US Navy during WWII and was stationed out in San Francisco, California. Mother took a train out to marry him. She got a wonderful job at a federal reserve bank. She told me she used to see movie stars all the time who would come in and cash their bonds. My father learned how to do sheet metal work.

Now back to my story about Nan. As it turned out, years later one Thanksgiving, Nan's son and his wife were coming home to visit with her. By this time, my grandfather, Doug had passed away and she was a widow for the second time. Austin and his wife were coming around a bad curve in the mountains of Kentucky when a large coal truck slammed into them head on. The accident decapitated Nan's son, Austin and both of them were killed instantly.

Later on, when Nan grew old and was alone, she developed horrible crippling arthritis. She called my father's sisters and asked if they would let her come to live with them. They all said, "No. You never wanted us when we were little, now we don't want you when you need us!" Tell me that you don't reap what you sow! It is a dangerous thing to mistreat a child. *Take heed that ye despise not one of these little ones; for I say unto you,*

that in heaven their angels do always behold the face of
my Father which is in heaven. (Matthew 18:10)

Because of the way my grandfather neglected my father and turned his back on him in that he would not stand up to Nan, my father was bitter his whole life. I never dreamed that my father was the son of a pastor. He had backslidden when I was about four and I never saw him pray or show any signs of being a Christian. I always wondered why he was so mean at times and then when I was about 15 my mother told me about his horrible childhood. My father told us that he would never forgive Nan, even if it meant he would die and go to hell. After my mother and I were saved, we prayed for my father to be able to forgive Nan and be saved. Sadly it was not until the very end of his life that he forgave her. He finally realized she had paid for her sin.

Getting back to David and me. When my husband resigned the church, he didn't know what in the world he would do for a living. He started evangelizing at various churches for love offerings. It became apparent very quickly that we could not survive on love offerings as some churches didn't give him enough to pay for his travel expenses, let alone extra. It became clearer and clearer that David was going to have to get a secular job in order to provide for our family.

One time David preached at a certain church of about 600.The pastor's wife asked him why he was traveling as an evangelist instead of pastoring. David told her about my health. She confided to David that she had been suffering from horrible depression and wished her husband would do what David did, but her husband never did leave the church. More than likely it is because he didn't know what else to do for a living. Many pastors' wives feel like they cannot go on wearing a mask for the church anymore and they split. There is so much pressure on the pastor's family.

When our daughter was very young she began asking me if her daddy was dead because David was gone on the road so much, traveling as an evangelist. We both hated being apart so much that we began asking God to provide for us another way. David and I began praying for God to make a way for him to come off the road. Soon afterwards, my husband got a job through a friend selling manufactured homes in Richmond, Kentucky. It was there that he learned how to do financing. Little did we know that God was setting us up for bigger and better opportunities.

After David was there for awhile, he wanted to be closer to our sons who were living in Florida. One of our former board members told David about another job located in Florida at a mortgage company. The board member highly recommended David for the job and he got hired. We were so thrilled to have our whole family back together again. Then a few years later, a co-worker left the company and went to work for a bank. She knew they were looking for mortgage lending officers and so she recommended David for that job. Once again, we can look back and see how the hand of the Lord has been upon us every step of the way. David was hired and eventually they promoted him to first vice-president of residential lending. God has been so faithful to us. He made a way of escape that I could bear my life. His ultimate goal was for me to receive my complete healing. I was finally going to be able to just "be" and not "do" as I had prayed so many years before.

In all thy ways acknowledge him, and he shall direct thy paths.

(Proverbs 3:6)

CHAPTER 11:

PROPER DIAGNOSIS

The National Institute of Mental Health describes manic depressive illness as involving episodes of serious mania and depression. One of the leading researchers of manic depressive illness told me that it is an <u>energy disorder</u>. That explains why a person with this illness will feel like taking on ten projects one day and never finishing them; because they run out of energy. Getting properly diagnosed of manic-depressive disorder, more commonly called bipolar disorder is very difficult. In my case, I never had extreme highs. I also never had the classic symptoms of bipolar disorder. I primarily suffered from debilitating, chronic depression that was later diagnosed with being bipolar II disorder.

You will need to have a series of tests to rule out other causes which can precipitate depression. Brain tumors, head injuries or a concussion to the head, thyroid conditions and genetics are common factors to be taken into consideration. Even poor nutrition and hormone imbalance can cause a person to feel depressed. One woman got on antidepressants and her depression grew worse. Come to find out, she later learned she had diabetes. Not everyone suffers with the same symptoms in the same way. There is a lot of gray area with mood disorders.

Most people will put off getting medical treatment because they keep thinking the depression will eventually lift when their circumstances change. In some cases, if the individual does not have a manic-depressive disorder or severe debilitating clinical depression, their depression may lift, once the sky turns blue again. Some people put off getting tests done because of the stigma that our society has attached to mental illness. Some act as though it is contagious. Unfortunately some bipolar people have displayed such despicable behavior that they have brought this stigma on themselves. Many have ruined marriages and relationships because of their mood swings and irrational behavior.

Fortunately not everyone who suffers from mental illness acts the same way and most can function normally if they are on proper medication. If you have manic depressive disorder and you refuse to get help because of you are in denial or think you cannot afford to see a doctor, you need to think again. If your automobile broke down, you would take out a loan or do whatever you needed to do to get it fixed. And if you are abusing a loved one or your family because of a clinical imbalance of your brain chemistry, you must understand that you cannot fix yourself and others will eventually grow weary of your verbal abuse or other negative behavior patterns. It may cost you your marriage, your job or --even worse-- your life, if you don't get medical treatment and counseling.

One of the first things your family doctor or psychiatrist will want to do is order a blood test to check out your thyroid and hormones, especially if you are a woman who may be going through menopause. There are several reasons that a person may be depressed and you first need to eliminate some physical issues.

If you have a physical condition that is throwing your hormone levels out of balance, you will suffer hot flashes and may even begin to suffer extreme depression and panic attacks. I felt like I was losing my mind before I got on the hormone crème. I cannot over emphasize the importance of getting your hormone levels checked out if you are a woman suffering from depression. When I went to my female doctor she told me my hormones were fine but I was still having problems with hot flashes and other symptoms so I ordered a wonderful hormone Menopause Moisture Creme that is all natural progesterone and it helps me tremendously with hot flashes and other hormonal symptoms. I get my crème from Daystar Television Network. Premarin comes from a pregnant mare's urine and has all kinds of side effects, especially weight gain. You want to make sure you use bio-identical hormones to prevent cancer and other side effects which you can learn about on the internet.

Low thyroid causes you to have fatigue and can also cause depression. A doctor can prescribe generic forms of thyroid pills that will also do wonders for a person. You will need to get those two tests out of the way first before you can determine if your depression is brought about by a traumatic experience, or if indeed it is a genetic cyclical case of some form of bipolar disorder. Most of us have low iodine levels and these affect our thyroid. The chemicals like fluoride and chorine deplete us from iodine so it is not enough just to get it from table salt. Magnesium and DHEA are other minerals we need to make sure we are feeling optimal.

There are no lab tests or x-rays that can confirm manic-depressive illnesses. The diagnosis rests in the hands of a knowledgeable and experienced psychiatrist and is usually determined by exclusion. Some people suffer from extreme highs and suicidal lows while others have what is called "mixed states".

Wikipedia says that Mania is the signature characteristic of bipolar disorder and, depending on its severity, is how the disorder is classified. Mania is generally characterized by a distinct period of an elevated mood, which can take the form of euphoria. People commonly experience an increase in energy and a decreased need for sleep, with many often getting as little as 3 or 4 hours of sleep per night, while others can go days without sleeping. A person may exhibit pressured speech, with thoughts experienced as racing. Attention span is low, and a person in a manic state may be easily distracted. Judgment may become impaired, and sufferers may go on spending sprees or engage in behavior that is quite abnormal for them. They may indulge in substance abuse, particularly alcohol or other depressants, cocaine or other stimulants, or sleeping pills. Their behavior may become aggressive, intolerant, or intrusive. People may feel out of control or unstoppable, or as if they have been "chosen" and are "on a special mission" or have other grandiose or delusional ideas. Sexual drive may increase. At more extreme phases of bipolar I, a person in a manic state can begin to experience psychosis, or a break with reality, where thinking is affected along with mood. Some people in a manic state experience severe anxiety and are very irritable (to the point of rage), while others are euphoric and grandiose.

To be diagnosed with mania according to the Diagnostic and Statistical Manual of Mental Disorders (DSM), a person must experience this state of elevated or irritable mood, as well as other symptoms, for at least one week, less if hospitalization is required.

Severity of manic symptoms can be measured by rating scales such as self-reported Altman Self-Rating Mania Scale and clinician-based Young Mania Rating Scale.

The best way to distinguish if a person is suffering from manic-depressive disorder is by looking at their family history. By and large this disease is genetic, but not everyone who suffers from depression is bipolar or has a mood disorder.

Sometimes depression is caused from a great loss or traumatic experience but the individual may still need some antidepressants on a short term basis to get them over the hump but the most important thing to do is to get therapeutic counseling. I believe many a person would not need antidepressants to mask their depression if they would get Christian counseling.

Regardless of the type of depression you have, there needs to be a correct diagnosis from a qualified caring psychiatrist. I prefer Christian psychiatrists, if you can possibly find one, since they will not try to blame your religious beliefs for your depression and they also recognize there is a higher power who can give them guidance when trying to find a proper medication for treatment. I was blessed to find one who would even pray with me before and after our sessions. I have also been to one psychiatrist who gave me Adderall. After we moved, the new psychiatrist would not give me Adderall as he said it would cause a manic episode. You need to research every single drug that you take online and read the reviews to make sure they will not inter-act with each other or cause you to have a manic epi-sode. If you are pregnant, some of the antidepressants can cause birth defects.

A merry heart doeth good like a medicine: but a broken spirit drieth the bones.

(Proverbs 17:22)

CHAPTER 12:

⚜

SIGNS OF DEPRESSION

I have tried to list some of the classic signs of depression in the order that they tend to follow. Not everyone who has manic-depressive disorder or severe depression will have them all or in this order but you will need to pay close attention if you notice this pattern developing:

- Racing thoughts
- Inability to concentrate
- Feelings of anxiety, worry and fear
- Sleeping too much or having an inability to sleep
- Eating too much or not eating enough
- Little to no energy
- Failure to bathe, dress and do menial tasks that one normally has in the past

- Lack of sexual desire
- Withdrawal from life, isolation from normal activities
- Staying in the house in a darkened room
- Feelings of overwhelming guilt
- Feelings of worthlessness, lack of self-esteem
- Feelings of hopelessness
- Feelings of wanting to run away
- Attempting suicide

One of the first signs of depression is a general feeling of malaise and loss of interest. You may think that You are tired or having a bad day. You don't feel like getting out of bed or talking with people. Maybe you had a conflict with a friend or co-worker and you just feel down. Maybe something went wrong with your hopes and dreams and you had a major disappointment in life. Whatever caused the trauma, a normal person will grieve for his or her loss and then get on with life in due time. All of us feel like this from time to time, which is perfectly normal. However, when you continue to feel generally tired all day long and don't feel like being around people or going anywhere for an extended amount of time, you need to talk with a doctor and a counselor.

People who have manic-depressive disorder may not have had a traumatic experience at all and have no explanation for their depression. Quite the contrary, they may feel guilty because they have so many reasons to be happy with their lives. Their depression is abnormal. Depression that lingers and progressively grows worse is a big red flag, even if you have suffered from a major loss in your life.

Even "normal" people who are not bipolar may experience some degree of depression if they lose a close member of the family, a good friend or their job. Even a move can trigger depression. However, if the depression lingers for longer than a few weeks and the depression begins to interfere with their way of life to the point that you cannot function normally any longer, you need to seek out medical help.

You may not recognize depression at first it is so subtle. When others begin to see your personality changing from an outgoing, fun loving person into a recluse who hardly wants to get dressed or out of bed, they need to take some affirmative action on your behalf and encourage you to get to a doctor at once and seek counseling and medical treatment before the condition progresses into the next stage.

The second stage usually progresses from a general lack of energy and interest to a more serious state of lethargy and withdrawal from activities and life in general. At this point you may find you don't want to go out to work or with friends and family or shopping or engage in any of your hobbies that you once enjoyed. I had always adored horses but in this state if someone had put one in the living room I wouldn't have been able to go and see it. I had no interest in any of the things that I had always enjoyed and no energy to perform even the smallest of tasks.

You have a difficult time concentrating and making even the slightest decisions. I couldn't decide on what to order at a restaurant. I couldn't work anymore because I couldn't concentrate and I had the "dead look" in my eyes all of the time. If you have suffered from depression or have had loved ones who have suffered from long periods of deep depression, you will learn to recognize this "look" in their eyes. I have even seen it in dogs and horses eyes. The eyes are a window to the soul. Some cannot hide the depression in that way. They may smile but you can even see it in pictures.

I had my photo taken at the beach and my husband pointed out to me that he could see "depression" in my eyes, even though I was smiling. He wanted to have a new one taken after I was healed and you could see the obvious difference.

In the second stage, you may find that even the most menial of tasks seems like a monumental drudgery. I noticed that in this stage I could barely drag myself out of bed to get dressed and brush my teeth or take a shower.

Having company was also stressful. I knew I had to try to put on my mask and try to hide my depression. Who wants to hear about it? You know the saying, "Laugh and the whole world laughs with you. Cry and you cry alone." The more you talk about feeling depressed, especially to the wrong person, the more they can make you feel worse; if they don't understand and try to make you feel guilty.

I found that most of the time if I tried to express my feelings to others, I felt worse. People who have never experienced clinical depression can not relate nor empathize. Some were extremely judgmental and condemnatory. Sometimes people think you are crying for attention and feeling sorry for yourself. While that may be true for some, I and the people that I have known who have suffered from bipolar disorder are embarrassed, ashamed and feel very guilty about their feelings. They abhor themselves and for the most part will try to hide the fact that they are feeling so low from others.

Then the last stage is when you feel totally hopeless and like life will never get any better. You feel as though you are in "a black hole" with no light at the top. You feel catatonic, zombie like, just going through the motions. Even getting to the restroom takes every ounce of energy you can muster. You begin to think about suicide because you feel like that is the only way to find peace and joy again. You have looked at your shortcomings and your situation a million times and feel there is no hope. You compare yourself to others and feel totally worthless as a human being.

I began to think about how much better off my family would be without me and how much better off I could be if only I had the nerve to kill myself and I could go to heaven.

I personally don't see how anyone who is not a believer in Christ makes it through this last stage. Jesus is the only way I made it through these years of being there and I now realize He was with me and carried me through until He set me free. You can bet that when you are in this condition, the enemy will come and tempt you to end your life.

I would have to get my husband to pray with me for hours in order to ward off the demonic voices in my head. They were not audible but the thoughts were no doubt from him. If you have ever been there, you know what I am talking about. Most people who end up in this stage end up getting on massive doses of anti-depressants and having electroconvulsive therapy (ECT). I was never hospitalized like my mother and grandmother had been numerous times, nor did I ever have to undergo ECT as they had. I am so thankful that God gave me the grace to make it through with the medications and the support of a wonderful, godly, praying Christian husband.

I am not against using anti-depressants and neither should any one be, if you or your loved one has to use them to get them through life. Otherwise, I would have become catatonic and non-functional. I wouldn't be here today if it had not been for the meds and counseling all of those years. The problem is that medical science can only do so much and these drugs are usually accompanied with several side effects. Most of them will affect your libido and make you sleepy and tired all of the time. Many of them will make you gain weight and feel "spacey", unable to concentrate. But as my doctors told me, it would be better to get on the medications than to commit suicide.

When I first got on the medications, all I wanted to do was sleep. David and I went to visit some good friends and I remember lying in the floor and falling asleep on their carpet. I was so embarrassed but couldn't stay awake no matter how much tea or coffee I drank. As time went on, I was able to change to a different type of medication and I felt much better and was even able to work.

I would like to warn anyone who is thinking about getting on anti-depressants to do some research on the internet first. Read other peoples reviews and study their side effects and withdrawal symptoms. Some of them are nearly impossible to get off of and I strongly recommend that you avoid those. A friend of mine was given Klonopin and he said that if he had known how hard it was to get off of and the side effects, he would never have started it. So whatever you are prescribed, make sure you search the internet for every bit of information you can find about the drug.

Most antidepressants will affect your libido. I have had several people confide in me that their relatives were divorced because they could no longer enjoy sex on the antidepressants. I can only suggest that you both try to meet each other's sexual needs as much as possible and talk with your doctor. You have to work at your marriage no matter who you are and when you are suffering from depression it is extremely hard to want to become intimate. However, the last thing you want to do is give the enemy place in your bedroom. Touch each other, compliment each other, kiss each other and do whatever you have to do to keep your marriage from going cold. Again, there are wonderful Christian and I do stress Christian counselors out there that you need to avail yourself of if at all possible. As I said before, many times you can deal with your emotional issues and avoid antidepressants. There are new antidepressants that are coming out on the market that do not affect the libido as much as some of the old ones. Again, some drugs are so highly addictive that they are nearly impossible, if not impossible to come off of if you are on them even a short amount of time. By all means, if you want to come off of an antidepressant you need to work closely with a psychiatrist. If you do research on the internet about the withdrawal side effects you will realize that many have committed suicide by trying to come off too quickly.

Only take antidepressants as a last resort and try to remain on them only for a short period of time. The longer you are on them the harder it is to come off of them. In looking back over my life, I believe if I had worked closely with a Christian counselor, I would not have stayed on antidepressants for so long. I just didn't realize how to come off them and I didn't know how to stand on God's word for my healing in faith. I didn't realize my authority as a believer even though I had been a Christian for so long and I had some emotional issues that were not being dealt with.

After having been a pastor for 25 years and seeing all of the broken lives in my own family, I realized early on how important it is that we don't try to put a band aid on a broken heart. If you have hidden hurts and old wounds that have never been healed, you must get those healed before you will be able to get your mind healed. Jesus wants us whole. He wants us free and He will work with us for as long as it takes to get us that way.

But unto you that fear my name shall the Sun of righteousness arise with healing in his wings; and ye shall go forth, and grow up as calves of the stall.

(Malachi 4:2)

CHAPTER 13:

❦

SAD (SEASONAL AFFECTIVE DISORDER)

One of the things I noticed was that I seemed to suffer more from depression in the fall and winter seasons, even after we moved to Florida. If you are like me, than more likely you have a condition known as Seasonal Affective Disorder (SAD). Symptoms range from lack of energy, weight gain, craving of sweets and a desire to sleep more often. Usually these symptoms begin during the fall when there is not as much sunlight and resolve in late spring when the days grow longer. People who work inside without any windows may be inclined to suffer from SAD.

People who suffer with SAD say that their symptoms come and go about the same time every year. The symptoms include:

- Depression
- Weight gain
- Difficulty concentrating
- Withdrawal socially
- Loss of energy
- Oversleeping
- Change in appetite
- Anxiety

In the early 1980's, Neal Owens was diagnosed with Seasonal Affective Disorder (SAD) – a newly identified medical disorder characterized by winter symptoms which included fall and winter weight gain, carbohydrate cravings, oversleeping, decreased interest in normal activities, and low mood and energy.

He contacted the National Institute of Mental Health (N.I.M.H.), as they were conducting investigations into treating this newly identified problem with an experimental treatment called "bright light therapy." Though he didn't qualify to participate in the program (he was excluded because he was taking antidepressant medications at the time), the researchers allowed him to borrow one of their light boxes so he could try it on his own.

Two weeks later, when he was asked to return the light box to N.I.M.H. for their study; he was convinced of its efficacy in treating his symptoms. He asked where he could buy one, and the researchers told him there were none available commercially – they had jury-rigged the units they were using.

So Neal made his own, using specifications for brightness and safety provided to him by the researchers. When they saw Neal's SunBox, which was superior to their light boxes, they asked him to work with N.I.M.H. to develop a light box for their research that was safe, durable and effective.

As people left the study at N.I.M.H., those who responded well to bright light therapy were referred to Neal so they could special-order SunBoxes for their use at home. This is how The SunBox Company began. Founded in 1985, they were incorporated in 1987. Not only are they the original bright light box company, but they are recognized worldwide as a leader in light therapy products. (used by permission by Frank Kall, The SunBox Co., 2011)

I purchased a SunBox desk lamp which helps me tremendously with SAD and withdrawals from the antidepressants. I use it for 30 minutes in the morning and I can feel a big difference in my energy level and overall feeling.

The people that walked in darkness have seen a great light: they that dwell in the land of the shadow of death, upon them hath the light shined.

(Isaiah 9:2)

CHAPTER 14:

❦

LASER LIGHT THERAPY

Medical science has been making some major breakthroughs using laser light therapy. There are clinical studies being done with this technique and I strongly believe that the next focus on healing depression will be with **laser light therapy** also know as acupuncture laser therapy. If you or someone you know is suffering from severe depression, before you start taking antidepressants, find someone near you who is using laser light therapy. Check with your nearby universities to see if they are doing a clinical study where you can participate and save some money.

The World Health Organization (WHO) now recognizes acupuncture as a complimentary treatment for depression.

It is important to understand that according to researchers, lower levels of serotonin in individuals can make an individual prone to addiction, depression crime, etc. The reason for some individuals having lower levels of serotonin has not yet been determined. These same researchers hypothesized that it could be genetically related, but the environment, in the form of a physical or emotional trauma could possibly trigger it.

Many believe that the reason acupuncture (laser therapy) helps to relieve depression is because it stimulates the release and synthesis of serotonin.

Acupuncture (laser therapy) also causes the release of endorphins in humans and noradrenaline-norepinephrine in animals. In general, "increased levels of serotonin and endorphins are consistent with emotional well-being."

Many other scientists acknowledge the need for more research in this area in order to establish the exact mechanisms of these neurotransmitters, and how they are linked to acupuncture (laser therapy). After reading through many studies it seems that several scientists are willing to acknowledge the use of acupuncture as a treatment for depression.

Many studies even report that acupuncture is as effective in treating depression as antidepressants. According to researchers traditional treatments for depression, such as psychotherapy and pharmacology, work for roughly 50% of the patients who finish the treatment. There are many patients however, who do not finish these treatments because of unbearable side effects or disillusionment with their medication or psychotherapy treatments.

More research definitely needs to be done to better understand acupuncture's (laser therapy) effect on depression, but it looks like acupuncture (laser therapy) can develop into a very promising treatment for depressive disorders. Laser therapy may not work for all patients, but is is definitely worth trying, since **it is painless, inexpensive and free of side effects**. (Used by permission from Imaginelaserworks, Ralph Semple, 2011)

The Spirit of the Lord GOD is upon me; because the LORD hath anointed me to preach good tidings unto the meek; he hath sent me to bind up the brokenhearted, to proclaim liberty to the captives, and the opening of the prison to them that are bound;

(Isaiah 61:1)

CHAPTER 15:

❧

GENETICS AND DEPRESSION

My Mother had a complete hysterectomy at the age of 42 and she had her first nervous breakdown soon after that. My father had always blamed her breakdown on her hysterectomy; but after I began to suffer with depression, I began to do some research and learned it can be genetic. In fact, I will never forget the time I went to visit my mother in the hospital during one of her nervous breakdowns and I asked the doctor what was causing them. He said, "Genetics. Do you know anyone in her family that has a history of mental illness?" I said, "Her mother, my grandmother, has had some nervous breakdowns, and my grandmother's father committed suicide because he was so depressed." Then I asked, "Well, great! What are the chances of my brother, sister and me having a nervous breakdown?" He said, "30%."

My maternal grandmother, Gay Roller Bays.

I cannot tell you how fearful I became in that instant. I had already been battling severe prolonged periods of post partum depression. When the doctor made that statement, I felt hopeless, terrified and thought there was nothing I could do. I felt like I was being pulled by a strong undercurrent downstream towards Niagara

Falls and there was absolutely nothing I could do to keep from falling over the edge. All the way home I kept hearing the doctor's words, over and over in my mind. From then on it was like waiting for a time bomb to go off in my body. I knew it was ticking but just didn't know how long it would be before I would sink into the sea of hopelessness and total despair. It wasn't long before the bomb went off and I went over the edge. It would be many years before I could ever find my way out of, "the black hole".

I know now that I do not have to believe the negative report. As a believer we should declare the report of the Lord and His report says we are healed. *Finally, brethren, whatsoever things are true, whatsoever things are honest, whatsoever things are just, whatsoever things are pure, whatsoever things are lovely, <u>whatsoever things are of good report;</u> if there be any virtue, and if there be any praise, <u>think on these things. (Phil 4:8)</u>*

I have been raising Cavalier King Charles Spaniels for 16 years. Recently, I sold a puppy to a husband and wife and we began talking about my book. The wife told me that her mother had spent most of her entire life in mental institutions. I asked, "Had she been abused?" and this lady said, "Absolutely not! She was raised on a plantation and treated like a princess!" She went on to say, "We believe it runs in her side of the family."

If you are suffering from depression, look thoroughly into your family tree. Unfortunately, oftentimes people who are depressed will try to drown their sorrows with drugs and alcohol which only makes the problem far worse since alcohol is a depressant.

Even if you have inherited bipolar disorder, there are several things you can do to overcome the depression as I have written in my book. You don't have to feel like it is a death sentence and there is nothing you can do about it. There is hope for you today and medical science is making progress in giving alternatives to antidepressants.

For by thy words thou shalt be justified, and by thy words thou shalt be condemned.

(Matthew 12:27)

CHAPTER 16:

৩৬৩

WORDS CAUSE DEPRESSION

I believe that one of the primary reasons people suffer from depression is because of the breakdown in the home and the words that have been spoken over them. ***Death and life are in the power of the tongue, and those who love it will eat its fruit. (Proverbs 18:21)*** We have to be extremely careful what we speak over our children because our words literally can make or break them.

When our daughter was a baby, David and I used to constantly affirm her and tell her how smart and beautiful she was. We didn't want her to ever feel like she was a second class member of our family because she was adopted. We always told her we loved her and wanted to make sure she had opportunities to develop her God given gifts.

When she was barely able to talk she would sing the Barney song, "I wuv you, you wuv me, we're a happy family." One of the cutest things she did was to go around telling everyone, "I so smart!" David and I showered her with love but we also set boundaries and gave her responsibilities. We didn't want her to grow up feeling sorry for herself because she was adopted and we didn't want to spoil her rotten like the girl was that I had known that abused her horses.

We taught her to be a leader, not a follower. Today, by the grace of God, she has turned out to be a fine young Christian lady. She is working as a waitress while putting herself through nursing school. I cannot tell you how many times her school teachers and employers have commented on how self-assured and confident she is. She has never given us one minute's problem with drugs or alcohol. But what if we had never affirmed her and verbally abused her and told her she would never amount to anything?

My mother had a younger brother and sister-in-law who were horrible alcoholics and they had two sons. They fought like cats and dogs. One time I saw my uncle get drunk and hold an iron to my aunt's face. They became increasingly violent toward each other and fought in front of their sons. My uncle could not

keep a job because of his drinking. His wife was unfaith-
ful to him. One time my uncle came in the house and
found his wife trying to drown their sons in the bath
tub. It was a horrible home life beyond anything I had
ever seen.

One Easter Sunday, my mother took my brother
and me to Sunday School. I was about eleven and my
brother about seven. We were all dressed up in our new
clothes and shoes. Mom and dad worked extremely
hard and God had blessed them beyond their wildest
dreams.

My mother and father didn't have a perfect marriage but it was a fairy tale compared to her brother's. After church, I can vividly remember this particular Easter going to my uncle's apartment. The
place reeked with the smell of alcohol and cigarettes.
There were beer cans, liquor bottles and cigarette
butts everywhere. Their apartment was cold and
dark because they could not afford to pay their electric bill. My aunt and uncle were passed out in the
bed drunk.

My cousins were only 10 and 12 at the time but
they had washed their clothes in cold water in the sink
because their parents did not do the laundry and there
was no hot water or electric. It was so pitiful. I felt guilty

for having nice clothes and having such a nice home compared to theirs.

The principal of the school called my mother and told her that one of my cousins, the ten year old, had been seen crying with his head on his desk because of all of the emotional stress he was under. The principal asked my mother if she would assist in having my cousins removed from their home and placed in a Boys Ranch. This was like an orphanage for boys. My mother, being the compassionate woman she was, agreed to do so. The courts proceeded and later my cousins were sent to the Boys Ranch. I cannot tell you how traumatized they were.

We would visit them on a regular basis but they were deeply affected. It is no wonder that a few years later one of them became an alcoholic and the other one a drug addict at a very young age. They suffered their whole lives from a low self-esteem and they never recuperated from the effects of their home life.

After my cousins were taken away, my aunt left my uncle and moved away and remarried soon after. She never had anything more to do with her sons.

My uncle began working at a bar and never stopped drinking. Later my parents took Darrell and my sister and her husband took Barry into our homes. I noticed that whenever my uncle came around he never had a kind word to say to either one of his sons. He would say things like, "Watch him, he can't walk across the room without tripping over his own two feet!" On and on my uncle would go with absolutely nothing but negative, belittling comments like that. He never gave either of them a kind word and I never saw him hug them or even touch them.

My cousins tried to drown out their miserable lives with drugs and alcohol. One died very young with AIDS and the other died with cirrhosis of the liver. Both of them were married and had children but their marriages failed. In fact my oldest cousin was married five times. Like their parents, they both abused their children and abandoned them. Their children didn't want anything to do with them when they became adults.

Exodus 34:7 talks about generational curses that come down the bloodline if we don't break them.

Keeping mercy for thousands, forgiving iniquity and transgression and sin, and that will by no means clear the guilty; visiting the iniquity of the fathers upon the children, and upon the children's children, unto the third and to the fourth generation. The only way you can break generational curses is to invite Christ into your life and live for Him.

To my knowledge, my cousins were not bipolar, but they suffered from depression because of the word curses they had heard their parents speak over their lives, time and time again. When a person keeps replaying the messages they have heard over and over in their minds, they become depressed and need spiritual counseling to get them free of the past. That is where the power of God's word comes in.

I had not been saved for too long when one particular morning I began to hear the voice of the Lord. Not audibly, but in my spirit. The Lord began to tell me that my beloved cousin was going to try to kill himself. His neighbor was involved with a cult and they told my cousin there was no hell; he would just burn up. I was sitting there listening to the voice of the Lord and I told the Lord that I had no idea where to find him because he had been robbing drug stores all around Kentucky and he was on the run. Then the Lord told me that he was at his father's fruit stand in Nicholasville. So I told David that I had to find out if indeed it was the Lord or if I was hearing voices.

I got into my Buick and began making the drive which was about an hour from our house in Richmond. Sure enough, when I got to the fruit market, there sat my cousin. He didn't even look surprised or shocked to see me. I asked if I could see him alone and we got in his father's truck. I told him that God had sent me and that God had told me he was going to kill himself. At first he flat out denied it. Then I got real serious with him and made him look at me. He began to break down and wept and said he couldn't take it anymore. His wife had left him and his world had fallen apart. I prayed under my breath, "Lord, what am I going to say?" Then I said, "How do you know there isn't a hell? If you take your life, and you end up in eternity burning in flames, you cannot come back." He knew that God has sent me and he came home with me for a couple of days. During that time he did pray with us and gave his heart to the Lord but I am sad to say that he went right back to the drugs. I do feel that before he passed away with AIDS he made everything right with the Lord. God gave me a scripture and right before he died, he called for a woman preacher to visit him in the hospital. God showed me it was because of me that he wanted a woman to come. David and I were in Florida and I came to visit him before he passed away but we couldn't come to his funeral. I know that he and his brother were saved and are in heaven. Praise the Lord!

When our son was young, he played soccer. At one of the games we noticed one of the fathers standing on the side lines with a video camera. He was constantly yelling at his son. His wife was sitting next to me. She was so upset because she could see how this man's verbal outbursts were affecting her son. All at once we saw this grown man take his camera and throw it on the ground as far as he could. His anger was off the chart over his son's performance at that soccer game. I have never forgotten how horrible I felt for that child and have wondered how his father's behavior affected him. Our words have power to heal, to soothe and to bless but they also have power to harm, to destroy and even to kill someone. Be careful what you speak over your children.

We have to learn the process of canceling out all of the old word curses of "death" and replace them with words of life that God's word says about who we are in Christ.

We have to learn that our significance and self-worth cannot come from what others think about us but who we are in Christ. I am convinced that I could have been healed years ago if I had truly understood these truths. As Christians, we have the authority to break the power of word curses and any other type of demonic strongholds from our past.

If you have haunting memories of negative words that were spoken over you, begin to declare what the Word says. Find scriptures that pertain to life and healing and put your name in there. *36If the Son therefore shall make you free, ye shall be free indeed. (John 8:36)* I can tell you that there is no greater power to heal than that of God's Word. Refuse to believe what someone else has spoken over your life if it is negative.

Blessed are the merciful: for they shall obtain mercy. (Matthew 5:7) [6]Nevertheless God, that comforteth those that are cast down.

(2 Corinthians 7:6)

CHAPTER 17:

LIVING WITH SOMEONE WHO IS DEPRESSED

Let me make it very clear that this is one of the most important chapters in this whole book. At the time of this writing, I have lived almost 60 years. I am writing from not only having lived with severe, chronic depression myself, but as I have already said in the previous chapters, my mother and grandmother both suffered with such debilitating depression that they had to be hospitalized and have electroconvulsive therapy (ECT). Not once, but several times over the course of their adult lives.

It seemed like my entire life depression robbed me from being able to enjoy my mother because she was either having a nervous breakdown or battling depression. She was alternately taking my grandmother to the hospital or checking herself in to get treatment.

The one thing that I have lived to regret many times over, is the way that our family treated my mother and grandmother. I know that God allowed me to suffer from this disease if for no other reason than to help others get through it and to get healed and delivered from depression. He doesn't want others to go through what my family and I have gone through because of sheer ignorance.

The Bible says, *"My people are destroyed because of a lack of knowledge"*. *(Hosea 4:6)* If we had known back then what we know now, we would not have treated my mother so horribly.

It takes a special God-kind of love, patience and forgiveness to hang in there with someone who is no longer living a productive and active life. We are as a whole, basically self-centered people who only want to associate with people who can make us feel good and benefit us in some way. There is a popular saying, "It's all about you." but I have learned that I am much happier when I am thinking about others. Especially those who feel alone and forgotten. It is a rare thing to be there for a person who is down and out and feels as weak as a newborn kitten. A person who is suffering from depression may be unable to give back to you at the time, but when you do reach out to them, and they begin to respond to your love, they will often flourish and remember your acts of kindness.

My mother was always working, doing, going and serving others when she was well. She was the oldest child and only daughter. She had a younger brother. Both of her parents were alcoholics. My grandmother had actually given birth to my mother when she was very ill. She only weighed 4 lbs at birth but the doctors said she had been bigger before my grandmother became so ill and stopped eating. I believe my grandmother had something similar to pneumonia right before she had given birth to my mother.

Mother was extremely gifted in several areas which seem to be a common denominator for people who suffer with bipolar illness. Ernest Hemingway, Vivian Leigh, Van Gogh and Patty Duke all suffered from debilitating highs and lows from manic depressive illness, more commonly knows as bipolar disease. When there was news about Mel Gibson's extreme erratic behavior, one of his doctors described his behavior as being classic bipolar. The doctor went on to say that so many manic depressives will self medicate with alcohol or drugs which only exacerbates the problem.

My grandmother and grandfather were both alcoholics. There has been some speculation that bipolar illnesses seems to run higher in number to children of alcoholics. My mother's depression started right after she had a complete hysterectomy at the age of 42. She and my father both worked as a team. He was the brawn and she was the brains. He had dropped out of school as an 8th grader to work at the tipple in the coal mines of eastern Kentucky. Later when my father joined the Navy, he learned how to work with sheet metal. When he got out of the service, he began working for a man in Lexington, Kentucky installing furnaces because he knew how to use sheet metal. Upon watching the builders of these new homes, he felt he had learned enough from observing them to step out on his own.

Mother was a brilliant bookkeeper and she also was a natural born saleslady. People used to say that she could sell a snowball to an Eskimo. She was also a fabulous interior decorator. When I was very young, I vividly recall her taking me into wallpaper stores. She would pour over wallpaper books for days while trying to match the paper to the right color of paint and carpet samples. She would take me to the lighting stores. She would spend weeks tying everything together. Several of the realtors said that my mother was one of the finest interior decorators they had ever seen. She was an amazing gifted mathematician too. She did all of my fathers payroll and drew up all of their sales contracts on their homes. She was the one who would show and sell the homes because she loved people so much and had a wonderful, outgoing, bubbly personality. As you can see from all of the work she did, she was extremely intelligent and a hard worker. God blessed my parents tremendously, and He made up for their horrible childhoods.

The point I am trying to make is that my mother was normally a giver and a hard worker. She didn't have a selfish bone in her body. No one worked any harder than she did. She loved to work. But when the depression hit her, it was like a freight train and she became totally bedfast and couldn't shower or dress herself. She would cry until she couldn't cry anymore tears. She stayed in her bedroom with her drapes closed and wouldn't go out. We had to take her to the hospital where they would administer electroconvulsive therapy (ECT) to her brain for several weeks.

When she came home, she usually had almost no memory. Fortunately, the ECT they use now is much safer than it was back then. Mom would be like a zombie for a few weeks. Eventually her memory would return and she would love her work again. Here is something I want to make sure you understand that she was not acting depressed so that we would feel sorry for her, nor was she just trying to get attention. She normally loved giving to others and she always loved her work when she was feeling well. When you have a friend or family member suffering from depression, there is nothing worse for their condition than for you to condemn them or accuse them of just wanting pity or sympathy.

What I found that helped me with depression was going out for a drive. I wrote about this in chapter one, when I first wanted to ride with David during that cold winter in Kentucky. If you are depressed or have a loved one who is depressed, try to take a ride to the beach or someplace you have not been before. Go someplace different that you may enjoy or just try to go to a movie or out to dinner. The more you get out of the house, the better you will feel. You don't need to stay isolated.

Usually people who are severely depressed want to be alone. You will need to coax them out of their comfort zone. If you can get them to drink a cup of coffee and bring them something to eat, this will help their metabolism. If you are a Christian, by all means offer to sit and pray for them. This helped me countless times.

Remember that people who are down and out and feeling severely depressed do not need to be forced to be with crowds. They are fragile and need your tenderness and patience. Never talk down to them. My husband would always speak kindly to me and assure me of his unconditional love. He would pay me compliments which made me want to fix up for him.

If your parent is depressed, tell him or her how much they mean to you. Tell them what a good parent they have been. If they have not been a good parent, then tell them you love them anyway and pray for them. Try to get them to church and help them with the chores that need to be done. Doing the slightest things around the house will help them feel better.

When I started feeling better, I joined the YMCA and began swimming and taking water aerobics. I felt so much better getting out in the sunlight and in the water. Exercise is wonderful for people who are depressed because it helps produce serotonin. Even if you just walk downtown or around your neighborhood, you will feel so much better.

Having a support group of friends is also essential. As I have said before, someone who suffers from depression usually wants to stay at home alone, but the best thing you can do to help yourself overcome depression is to be with people. The worst thing is for them to be alone.

Check to see if your church or another church has some kind of group that you can participate in such as a cell group, home Bible study or prayer meeting. There are all kinds of special interest groups in your community if you check in the newspaper. If you are able, check into volunteering at your local humane society, Hospice, hospitals, nursing homes, battered wife shelters and other organizations. Getting out of your house and feeling useful will help you tremendously. If you have a job that you have to go to, that also helps if it is not too stressful.

Getting a qualified Christian counselor is absolutely critical, if you can afford one. If you cannot afford a Christian counselor try to find a church that has one on their staff that you can see free of charge.

More than likely if you or someone you love is suffering from depression, it is because they feel "stuck" in a negative thought pattern of hopelessness. They need to learn how to renew their mind in the power of God's word and find there really is hope and things are not always going to feel so hopeless.

When someone has lost their mate or a close loved one, and they feel totally overwrought with grief, they will need time to heal. They also need to learn how to find meaning and joy again. They need to start rebuilding new memories. People deal with death in different ways. One person may want their loved one's photos everywhere while another person wants to take every photo and put them away. One person loves to talk about their loved one and another person cannot bear to mention his or her name. We each have to do what our heart says to do but we need to heal and be able to move on.

One of my friends told me that he decided to date soon after his first wife passed away because he played golf with a man who was still grieving the loss of his wife and she had passed away five years earlier. He said even though he dearly loved his wife, he realized he had to go on living and refused to allow himself to grieve like his golfing friend. As fate would have it, he married his wife's best friend who had lost her husband to cancer a year before he lost his wife. This older couple who were in their 60's was able to heal each other and move on forward with their lives.

Recently my brother-in-law lost his wife of 40 years to lung cancer. He and his wife got married when they were both 16 and had two children together. Naturally when his wife passed away he was devastated and he became severely depressed. The family prayed for him every day and it just looked like he had lost his will to live. My brother-in-law had always spoken to his neighbor who lived across the street from him, but they began hanging out with one another and traveling together. My brother-in-law is like a different person. He is still not ready to date anyone but at least he is not severely depressed and he now has his joy back.

Depression comes to us for different reasons and in different seasons. We have to learn how to re-program our minds and move beyond the past. Sometimes we need to make a change. If your job is making you sick, then try finding another one. If the weather where you live is making you sick, then begin praying and asking God to help you move someplace else. Whatever you are dealing with, God will help you if you trust in Him and wait for His perfect timing. In the meantime, try to focus on the positives you have in your life right now and see what you can do to improve your mental attitude while you are waiting. If you have a computer then you have the world at your fingertips. Don't allow yourself to feel hopeless. You have to fight in order to win the victory and overcome. Having unrealistic expectations can cause you to get depressed. So give God time and trust in His sovereignty. Learn to rest in Him by surrendering your will to Him.

The sacrifices of God are a broken spirit: a broken and a contrite heart, O God, thou wilt not despise.

(Psalm 51:17)

CHAPTER 18:

❧

DEPRESSION AMOUNG TEENS

On December 8, 2010, E Investigates had a special program dealing with suicide among teen-agers, "Exploring The Tragic Rise of Teen Suicides" by Laura Ling. According to her findings, every 40 seconds there is a suicide attempted by 10-24 year olds. Every 2 hours there is a suicide for the same age group. Suicide is the third leading cause of death for this age group.

There were different parents who were interviewed who had children who either committed suicide or attempted suicide. Every one of the children stated that they <u>hated themselves, felt hopeless, were too stressed and saw no way out of their situation.</u> We have to wake up and take notice of this epidemic among our young people.

Dr. Richard Lieberman, a school psychiatrist at the Los Angeles Unified School District, stated that there are two underlying factors contributing to these alarming statistics regarding these psychological issues: 90% of those who have committed suicide had some form of mental illness. 60% had mood disorders. Dr. Lieberman said that the mental illness is the fuel and when they had an acute situation that arose, the fuel was there to ignite potentially lethal situation.

Fortunately, counselors are much better trained now to detect a mental illness than they were years ago. One of the biggest problems, according to the doctors, is that there is such a stigma regarding mental illness that the children and teens **will do everything to hide their feelings. Teenagers feel the stigma a million times worse.**

Some of the teens on this show expressed that the reason they attempted suicide was because they felt ugly, fat, isolated, and useless. Some said they felt too much pressure from within and from their parents to be perfect. One boy committed suicide because his girlfriend broke up with him. **But they all said they wouldn't tell their friends or anyone their feelings because they were afraid of rejection from others.** Some of the tell-tale signs were self-mutilation, starvation, isolation, over sleeping, drinking alcohol or taking drugs. One of the girl's parents stated that they had noticed their daughter had become extremely angry when things didn't go just right. She had taken on too many activities after school and she put herself under pressure to be perfect in everything she did.

Most of the time, the teens would tell someone they were going to kill themselves, but their friends didn't take them seriously. Some will even give away there possessions. Some will leave notes.

If you have a child that is on antidepressants, he/she needs to be carefully monitored for any signs of depression. I found that several of the ones I tried actually made me much worse after time and the thoughts of suicide were there all the time. Only by the grace of God was I able to fight off the temptation to end my life because the pain was so horrible.

Never take it lightly if someone threatens suicide. There are parents who have lost their children because they did not realize how seriously they were depressed. If your loved one is catatonic and threatening suicide, you should talk to the doctor about having them committed to a hospital. Do not underestimate how serious depression can be. Marie Osmond just recently lost her son, who was suffering from depression, to suicide.

I went to school with a young boy who was just as cute as anything. His parents were constantly on his back to keep everything clean and neat at home and they never validated him. They both worked all the time. One day he called his girlfriend and told her that he was going to shoot himself. He said that his parents never loved him. He told her that he was going to get in the bathtub so that he wouldn't leave a mess for his parents to have to clean up. Before she could talk him out of it, the gun went off. He was only 16 years old.

If your loved one is talking suicide, take it very seriously and don't just say they want attention. If they need attention that bad, why do they have to threaten to end their life to get attention? If you have the ability to talk with them and show them love, by all means do so and try to get them to a therapist. Something has to be deeply traumatizing a person to reach this point of desperation. Take all guns out of the house and put them under lock and key. One of the most famous writers of all times, Ernest Hemingway was bipolar. He was severely depressed after having several series of shock therapy. The shock therapy which they administered back in his day, damaged his memory to the point that he couldn't write anymore and he took a shotgun and pulled the trigger with his toe. Everyone had begged his wife to remove the guns but she wouldn't.

Kristen Jane Anderson grew up in an all American family with a normal childhood. Her parents never divorced and everything seemed to be going fine. Then several things occurred that led her to the point of desperation. Her grandmother died, three of her friends died and another was dying of cancer, and then she was raped by her friend. She became very discouraged to the point that the feelings she felt inside simply overwhelmed her. On a cold January night, at the age of 17, Kristen attempted suicide by laying on a set of railroad tracks. She was run over by 33 freight train cars at 55 mph. Amazingly she lived but she lost both of her legs and 8 pints of blood. Afterwards, Kristen struggled with depression for another three years, but after accepting Jesus Christ and getting involved with a really good church, her life was transformed.

God helped her to get out of depression and off of all medications. Then she began speaking at schools and she started Reaching You Ministries (www.reachingyouministries.com). Kristen has written her powerful testimony, Life In Spite of Me which can be purchased on her website or Amazon.com She is helping thousands, if not millions of young people through her website, her book and her testimony. It is just so sad to think that a beautiful young 17 year old girl would feel so desperate that she actually laid on railroad tracks and tried to commit suicide. Thank God she was unsuccessful and today she is able to save others who are at that same point in their lives.

Recently, in our little town at our local high school, three students committed suicide. At another high school in Lake Co. a student wrote on the boys' bathroom wall that he was going to take his life. There was a total lockdown of the school and he didn't do it but obviously he was screaming for help.

The National Suicide Prevention Hotline phone number is (800) 237-8255 (Talk). If you, or someone you know is thinking about committing suicide, you need to call them immediately and seek out professional help. Suicide is 100% preventable.

But he was wounded for our transgressions, he was bruised for our iniquities: the chastisement of our peace was upon him; and with his stripes we are healed.

(Isaiah 53:5)

CHAPTER 19:

❦

HOW I RECEIVED SUPERNATURAL HEALING

As I have said, for 17 years, I was on anti-depressants and lived a fairly normal life. Despite all of the side effects, I worked, raised our children and took care of our home and even raised Cavalier King Charles Spaniels for 12 years. David and I continued to pray for my healing. Eventually, though, the drugs became completely ineffective and actually started making me feel suicidal again. This is very common with antidepressants and that is why you should be monitored very closely with your psychiatrist when you take them. Young people should especially be monitored because they are at a higher risk and they will hide their feelings more often than adults.

A series of events happened that looked like a disaster at the time but looking back on it now, David and

I can see it was all part of God's plan to get me off of antidepressants. We didn't know it, but my youngest son told me he had been praying for me to get off the medications. He saw how tired I was most of the time and how that I was unable to concentrate.

All of a sudden, I developed a cough which became so horrible that I would actually have spasms where I thought I was going to pass out. I coughed so hard that I became incontinent. My ribs hurt so badly I had to hold onto something when I stood up or lay down. I was in excruciating pain. My doctor put me on some steroids and other medications. The cough lasted for weeks and finally x-rays determined that I had asthma.

Then I began to have carpal tunnel problems. I was given shots of steroids in my wrists. Later I had surgery. All of the steroids combined with the anesthesia given to me for surgery, caused me to have a horrible hypo manic episode. Not until much later when my sister-in-law told me about Patty Duke's book, *A Brilliant Madness* did David and I finally learn that all of these steroids and the anesthesia were what caused me to have a manic episode. I had never had anything like this happen before. I became another person, totally unlike myself. I gave all of my beautiful breeding dogs away, which if you knew me that was totally unlike my character. Fortunately, I was able to get some of them back after several months. Then, I was cursing all the time. I don't mean little slips but I mean over the top cursing like I hated before. I also wanted to divorce my husband. He had neglected our marriage and I decided I wanted out so I left home for a while. This was totally out of my character. Then the guilt set in and I came back home. I told my husband that someone else was living inside my body and she was in control. It was a horrible feeling. I was constantly thinking of how I would kill myself. The depression was unbearable.

I went and had my will made out and told my husband that I couldn't take it anymore and that I was going to end my life. I knew the plan and this time I meant to go through with it. David knew I was serious and he began fasting immediately. He also began praying in tongues for hours. He would try to pray in the Spirit all night long. I was being tormented day and night with the demons of suicide.

Finally, one morning my youngest son told me to watch Sid Roth's program, *It's Supernatural*. Dr. Art Mathias founder of Wellspring Ministries in Alaska was his guest. Dr. Mathias began sharing about how that he was healed from an incurable illness and that many people who prayed the prayer he did were healed. He had my undivided attention. The prayer was simple: forgive others and forgive yourself.

I prayed the prayer along with Dr. Mathias but felt absolutely nothing. The next morning when I went to pour myself some coffee, the voice that I had come to know as the Holy Spirit softly whispered to me, *"You are breaking the second commandment in that you do not love yourself. You have never forgiven yourself." (Matthew 19:19)*

I began to meditate on what He said and God began to show me how much self-hatred I had. I was filled with self-loathing and self-condemnation. Truthfully, I had hated and despised myself since I was a little child. I was always comparing myself to others. This is one reason why it was so difficult for me to be a pastor. I always felt so inadequate and being a people pleaser was part of the job. If someone complimented me, I would hear them but could not receive it oftentimes, because I would follow up by thinking about all of my faults and past sins.

I remembered how callus I had been to my poor mother when she suffered from depression. There were things I had done as a child that I would still beat myself up over. I began to realize that my mother had a problem with the very same issue. Even in her eighties she would sit and cry over an abortion she had as a young woman.

My father had a vasectomy when he was in his 30's after they had three children. Amazingly, four years later my mother became pregnant. My father immediately accused her of having an affair. She had never loved anyone but my father and knew it was his child but how could it be? He went to the doctor and they showed him that his sperm test was completely normal.

When the doctors first began performing vasectomies, they just cut the tubes and did not cauterize or remove a section. Therefore, in some cases they actually grew back. My mother got it in her head that the baby would have something wrong with it. I know it was a spirit of fear and a spirit of abortion that hit her. But she didn't realize her authority as a believer and my mother and father were not walking with the Lord at that time. They were both consumed with building houses and trying to make a living.

Mother persuaded her doctor to perform a "therapeutic abortion" she confided to me. Immediately following this procedure, guilt began to overtake her. She cried for years and years and kept wondering what the child would have been like. Anyone who says that a fetus is a glob of tissue and they are going to feel better after having an abortion should have talked with my mother.

No matter how many times I would tell her the baby was with Jesus and in heaven, she would not be consoled. She had never forgiven herself and she kept on beating herself up for what she had done.

Now I realized that I was following in her footsteps. People with bipolar disorder have extreme mood swings and they also say and do things that they regret. Everyone does at some point in their lives; none of us is perfect, but people who have bipolar disorder have to pray earnestly for self-control or they will sabotage relationships they have by their actions and by their words. I had to go back and apologize to others for saying hurtful things. When my anger would get out of control, sometimes I would become obsessive compulsive. God guides, but Satan drives. I am so thankful that I am free from all of that now and that my wonderful husband had the love and grace to forgive me for my behavior.

This part of my story is one of the most important parts. If you read this and you don't get it, you won't benefit from this book. This process that God began to teach me was vital to my healing. I began forgiving myself any time and every time I would have a negative thought about something I had said or done in the past. I would not allow guilt and self-condemnation to keep me a prisoner any longer. It was a process that God began to teach me about toxic thinking and the power of my words—both negative and positive words. Proverbs 18:21 says, *Death and life is in the power of the tongue.* Proverbs 6:2 says, Thou art snared with the words of thy mouth, thou art taken with the words of thy mouth. When I was down, I would actually curse my body and pray to die. I would con- template killing myself. **These word curses gave Satan legal ground to keep me severely depressed. I was playing a dangerous game. I didn't realize how seri- ous my words against my own body were.**

No wonder I wasn't healed from depression when I would turn around and sabotage myself and undermine my own faith. God gives us a free will.

Our words are so powerful that God clearly says that whatever we say, we shall have. If we talk nega- tively, we will have negative effects. This has actually been proven scientifically. Dr. Caroline Leaf has stud- ied the brain for decades and her findings are aston- ishing about toxic thinking. She has written the book, Who Switched Off My Brain on the subject and I highly recommend it. When we allow negative thoughts to remain in our brain, they actually produce dead like looking trees. But the wonderful news is that when we refuse to allow these negative thoughts to remain in our brain, and replace them will positive thoughts, these dead looking branches will begin to grow back and flourish with life. Astonishing! Science is now able to prove what the Word says about our words and our thoughts.

The very next day, after I prayed with Dr. Art Mathias, I noticed that I didn't feel depressed. I wondered how long this feeling would last. **Daily, I had to learn how to speak positively to myself and I began repenting of everything that I had spoken negatively. I began to repent for speaking word curses over my body and instead, I began to bless my brain and bless my body.**

I began writing letters to people that I felt I had offended. I focused on forgiving others who had hurt and offended me. That was the hardest part but I knew that if I wanted complete healing I had to forgive others. Jesus makes that very clear.

Many people do not understand how to forgive. I didn't know how to forgive. When you make the decision to forgive you do not go by your feelings or emotions. You say with your mouth you for-

give the person for whatever it is they have done to you and then you line up your words with your confession just like you did when you got saved or received Christ as your personal Savior. In other words, let's say I choose to forgive _____ for _____. I don't feel any different right now. My heart tells me I still hate them. But if you will continue to confess that you forgave that person, it won't be long before your feelings will line up with your confession. When you pray you begin to pray a blessing upon them. You may not be able to think of anything else but bless them spiritually with the knowledge of Christ and His love. Pray for them to be filled with God's love. It doesn't happen instantly, it is a process. Every time the devil brings it up again, just bless them and remember to say that you have forgiven them and it will be gone. You have to forgive in order to be forgiven or you will be turned over to the tormentors the Bible says. You don't want the tormenting demons to harass you.

During this period, I also went to a wonderful place in Clearwater called The Healing House. Kathleen Peck is the pastor's wife and she and some of her church prayed with me. We have since become friends and I have attended her healing school. They helped me discover that the peace sign that I was wearing was an emblem of Satan. I did some spiritual house cleaning and removed everything in my house that I felt Jesus would not approve of. I had begun collecting various items with the peace sign on them such as jewelry, purses, clothing and had learned that this peace sign was a mockery of the cross. It is actually a cross that is broken and upside down. I researched this sign on the internet and found it listed under satanic symbols. Hitler and some of his high ranking officers had this peace sign on their headstones. Once I learned this truth about this peace sign, I got rid of everything I had with that sign on it. I didn't want anything that would grieve the Holy Spirit.

I also began casting down every thought that was negative. *Casting down arguments and every high thing that exalts itself against the knowledge of God, bringing every thought into captivity to the obedience of Christ. (2 Corinthians 10:5)*

As simple as this sounds, this my dear friend, is how my healing miracle began.

Another step that David and I took that helped bring about my healing was going to the beach. David and I had served as pastors for 25 years. During those years, we rarely ever got to do anything on the week-ends because David was consumed with preparation for Sunday services. We had neglected our marriage. The pastorate always came first. David realized this and he wanted to try to put some romance back into our marriage. He wanted to create some new memories. So my husband began taking me to Clearwater Beach nearly every week-end.

We began enjoying our new found life together. We felt like little children. We purchased two large floats and loved to put up our little umbrella and then launch out onto the beautiful warm gulf water. We would sit on our floats, hold hands and talk about our favorite past memories together. On the beach, children were building sand castles and enjoying quality time with their families

We had several close encounters with manatees, sting rays and dolphins. On one occasion, when I was coming out of the water, I accidentally stepped on a sting ray. It felt like someone plucked out a chunk of my foot with a pair of pliers. Immediately I was in excruciating pain! I ran onto the beach and sat there writhing in pain from the poison while David ran and got the car. He took me to the drugstore and got a sand bucket and filled it up with hot water and dishwashing soap. As soon as we put my foot in the bucket, the pain subsided. The barb indicated this was a large sting-ray and I learned very quickly how to shuffle my feet in the water to scare them away. But I couldn't let this event ruin our future trips to the beach. The sun helps the brain to produce serotonin, a natural anti-depressant.

I was pondering one day about why the sun and the water seemed to help lift my spirits and I remembered Psalm 23: *He leads me besides still waters. He restores my soul.*

After going for several days without feeling any depression, I wanted to see if God had indeed healed me. For at least 17 years I had tried dozens of different types of antidepressants. I began to step out in faith and wean myself off of all of my meds very slowly and methodically. I do not recommend that anyone else do what I did, but this is what I felt led to do. <u>Check with your doctor first. If you get off of your medications too quickly, you could end up in the hospital. It can be extremely dangerous.</u>

For a few days I would feel wonderful, and then the depression gradually began to creep back in again. I could not believe it. I asked the Lord what had happened to my healing? I had heard of people losing their healing because of unbelief but I had kept the faith. I asked God to give me wisdom and understanding about how to get my healing back. David and I had repeatedly stood on God's Word and exercised our faith. We had not waivered in our confession of faith. I believe that when God heals, he does it permanently and not temporarily. My husband began fasting again. Soon after that we realized that I was having major side effects from withdrawing from the Lexapro and Lithium.

Let me make it very clear, I believe that God uses doctors and medicine to bring healing. I will take it a step further to say that it does not mean that you do not have faith if you have to take medicine or go to the doctors. Three of the gospels record where Jesus said, _They that be whole need not a physician, but they that are sick. (Matthew 9:12, Mark 2:17 and Luke 5:31)_. Furthermore, Luke was a physician and he wrote the gospel of Luke in the New Testament. _Luke, the beloved physician, and Demas, greet you. (Colossians 4:14)_

God helped me to get off of all antidepressants, but when I tried to get off of Lithium, I couldn't. I would get severely depressed again and also begin have mood swings. I kept standing and standing on God's Word and finally one day I had a meltdown. I began weep-ing and I asked God what was wrong with my faith? I felt that I had been reading the Word, praying, fasting and doing everything His Word said to do. What was so frustrating was when I would hear others testify on TV about their healing I couldn't figure out what they had done that I had not done. I know that we are to *look unto Jesus who is the author and finisher of our faith.* (Hebrews 12:2)

Finally one day God spoke to me and he said, *"I am not against the doctors. I gave them their gifts. Medicine is my gift."*

I asked the Lord to confirm it with His word and I wanted New Testament scriptures. That is when He spoke, *"He that is whole needs not a physician but he that is sick."* And then the Lord reminded me of Luke, the physician who is in the New Testament.

I still take the Lithium but I am anticipating the day and hour when God tells me that I no longer have to take it. I know that by faith I am already healed, but until His healing is manifested, I have to take the medication. Lithium is not an antidepressant however it controls mood swings. It is a natural salt. It is one of the cheapest generic drugs Prescribed but has done miracles for me, and millions of others who are bipolar.

We do not have to beg God to heal us.

We do not have to beg God to heal us. I had been praying all wrong for most of my adult life.

I have learned now that Jesus already made provision for our healing when He bore those stripes upon His back. *Who his own self bare our sins in his own body on the tree, that we, being dead to sins, should live unto righteousness: by whose stripes ye were healed. (1 Peter 2:24)* **We just need to resist the symptoms in Jesus name.**

When it comes to getting off of medication, you need to have God confirm in your own heart that you are healed and you can get off of the medications. Otherwise this is presumption. God led me to get off of the antidepressants. I had to get off of the antidepressants because they were makin me suicidal. Everytime I tried to come off of the Lithium, I took a nose dive back into depression. When I begged God to show me what was wrong, He very clearly spoke to my heart that He uses medicine and that was the method He chose to bring about my healing. I don't understand why He didn't let me get off the Lithium, when He did the antidepressants. That is a mystery. But I am believing for my complete healing and every day I confess, "By His stripes I am healed". I resist the bipolar disorder in Jesus name and I just wait for the Holy Spirit to show me when I can come off the Lithium. In the meantime, I have been able to counsel others who are bipolar who were not taking Lithium and they have found healing through this marvelous drug. God works in mysterious ways.

There are those who will wear glasses or hearing aids and take all kinds of aspirin and other medicines until Jesus comes. **We need to thank God for these medications and the doctors but continue to bless our bodies and confess His Word over ourselves daily.**

I should have realized that it would take a long time to wean off the antidepressants, but I had no idea it was going to take a year. Don't be presumptuous and cut back on your own. You need to consult a psychiatrist before you try to come off antidepressants. You have to cut back on them a certain way and some of them are so highly addictive that if you stay on them too long you may never be able to come off of them. There are several Blogs about this on the internet that I highly recommend. I can tell you that some people would never have been able to have come off of all the antide-pressants if they had been on them for as long as I had.

Some would ask me if I was demon possessed, demon oppressed or was this disease genetic. I have asked this question a million times and all that I can say is that all disease has its origin from Satan and I do not believe that I was possessed, but I do believe that there was a demonic stronghold or generational curse that had to be broken since this disease goes back to my great-grandfather who actually committed suicide from depression. The Word talks about some diseases that go not out but by prayer and fasting. (Matthew 17:21). I only know that until my husband and I began to fast and pray in tongues and stand on the word daily, I was not able to get free.

I also believe that the enemy will try to steal whatever blessing God gives to us and we have to stand on God's word and His authority as believers in order to have complete and total victory. *The thief cometh not, but for to steal, and to kill, and to destroy: I am come that they might have life, and that they might have it more abundantly. (John 10:10)*

God sent his only son, Jesus, not only to save us from our sins so that we could have eternal life, but He also allowed him to suffer from the scourging with the stripes upon his back for our healing. I feel like the Psalmist David did when he penned these words*: O Lord…I pleaded with you, and you gave me health again. You brought me back from the brink of the grave, from death itself, and here I am alive?* (Psalm 30:2-3).

When God sets us free, we are free the Word says: *Whom the Son sets free, is free indeed! (John 8:36)*

God could have removed the depression, but He wanted me to be whole.

Beloved, God could have removed the depression but He wanted to remove the root cause of the depression. He wanted me to be every wit whole. I had to learn to stop hating myself, to love and forgive myself and others. I had to learn to deal with ungodly, negative, toxic thoughts that the enemy would bring to my mind or I would never be totally free and able to experience the abundant life that God has for me. There is no other religion in the world that has what we can have in Jesus Christ our risen Savior: total salvation from sin, sickness and demonic strongholds and everlasting life. He paid it all so that we can have it all.

DAVID'S DREAM

⚜

Right after I received my healing and David and I started going to Clearwater Beach, David had a marvelous dream. He said he and I were on the beach and it was a gorgeous day. The sun was shining and the waves were turquoise blue. The sand was powdery white. We both had a really dark tan. He and I were like two little kids. We were holding hands and walking beside the water and there were all kinds of marine life—dolphins and fish, turtles an all that seemed to be following us. All of a sudden I began skipping like a little girl, swaying my hips from side to side. He said the thing that he noticed the most was that my face was all aglow. I was so happy, like he had never seen me before. I was smiling from ear to ear because I was free at last! I know that God gave him this dream to encourage both of us.

God is the author and finisher of our faith

(Hebrews 12:2)

CHAPTER 20:

❧

MORE SCRIPTURES REGARDING HEALING

The greatest tool that I have used to heal my mind from depression is the power of God's word. Some of the scriptures that David and I quoted on a regular basis are:

Being confident of this very thing, that he who hath begun a good work in (me) you will perform it until the day of Jesus Christ. (Philippians 1:6)

⁷For God hath not given us the spirit of fear; but of power, and of love, and of a sound mind. (2 Timothy 1:7)

This is a scripture that I confess probably more than any other because of the fear that I have had to deal with. I also pray over my head and bless my brain daily.

³¹But they that wait upon the LORD shall renew their strength; they shall mount up with wings as eagles; they shall run, and not be weary; and they shall walk, and not faint. (Isaiah 40:31)

I also pray this scripture and I declare this promise that as I wait upon the Lord I shall renew my strength… I shall mount up with wings as eagles, I shall run and not be weary, I shall walk and not faint.

²And be not conformed to this world: but be ye transformed by the renewing of your mind, that ye may prove what is that good, and acceptable, and perfect, will of God. (Romans 12:2)

When you get depressed, all kinds of thoughts will enter your mind and you have to stand on this scripture: I am not conformed to this world, I am transformed by the renewing of my mind. I prove what is good, acceptable and the perfect will of God. If what you are thinking is contradictory to the word of God then refuse to think on it.

¹⁶For which cause we faint not; but though our outward man perish, yet the inward man is renewed day by day. (2 Corinthians 4:16).

My inward man is renewed day by day by the word of God and prayer.

²³And be renewed in the spirit of your mind; (Ephesians 4:23)

I pray for God to help me to renew the spirit of my mind daily because it all begins in the mind.

[10]And have put on the new man, which is renewed in knowledge after the image of him that created him: (Colossians 3:10)

Put on the new man (woman) that you are if you are a believer.

I pray this scripture and declare that God will keep me in perfect peace as I keep my mind on Him and trust in Him:

[3]Thou wilt keep him in perfect peace, whose mind is stayed on thee: because he trusteth in thee. (Isaiah 26:3).

[5]And the Spirit of the LORD fell upon me, and said unto me, Speak; Thus saith the LORD; Thus have ye said, O house of Israel: for I know the things that come into your mind, every one of them. (Ezekiel 11:5).

[5]Casting down imaginations, and every high thing that exalteth itself against the knowledge of God, and bringing into captivity every thought to the obedience of Christ. (2 Corinthians 10:5).

God knows everything that comes into our minds therefore He is fully able to help us to cast down imaginations and every high thing that exalts itself against the knowledge of God. We have to bring into captivity every thought to the obedience of Christ.

[8]Finally, brethren, whatsoever things are true, whatsoever things are honest, whatsoever things are just,

whatsoever things are pure, whatsoever things are lovely, whatsoever things are of good report; if there be any virtue, and if there be any praise, think on these things. (Philippians 4:8)

When we are depressed we cast down imaginations and begin to focus on the truth and those things that are of a good report. This is another one of my favorite scriptures that I stand on daily.

³⁷Jesus said unto him, Thou shalt love the Lord thy God with all thy heart, and with all thy soul, and with all thy mind. (Matthew 22:37)

When we learn to love the Lord with all of our heart we learn how to overcome every problem in life. We have to seek Him first.

But seek ye first the kingdom of God, and his righteousness; and all these things shall be added unto you. (Matthew 6:33)

It is God's will for us to have life and peace.

⁶For to be carnally minded is death; but to be spiritually minded is life and peace. (Romans 8:6)

The Holy Spirit knows how to intercede for us:

²⁷And he that searcheth the hearts knoweth what is the mind of the Spirit, because he maketh intercession for the saints according to the will of God. (Romans 8:27)

When you pray in tongues or the Spirit, the Holy Spirit makes intercession for us according to the will of God. There is power when we pray in tongues. This is a tremendous weapon to use against the enemy.

[20]*But ye, beloved, building up yourselves on your most holy faith, praying in the Holy Ghost. (Jude 1:20)*

I began to search out everything I could find on divine healing and watch Christian TV ministries that believed in healing. I refused to nurture doubt and unbelief. When I felt extreme depression and the doubt and unbelief began to hit me with such a force that I thought I would never feel better, in my weakened state my husband and I would begin to pray in tongues and quote God's words.

You may have never received the baptism of the Holy Spirit or the gift of tongues. I am going to try to explain why you need these gifts in order to do spiritual warfare and receive your healing. Jesus told his disciples to g0 *to Jerusalem and wait for the gift his Father had promised. He then told them that John (the Baptist) had baptized them with water but in a few days they would be baptized with the Holy Spirit. (Acts 1:4).*

This clearly indicates that there are two separate baptisms: the first one was in water and now the second baptism would be in the Holy Spirit. You receive the Holy Spirit when you are saved:

6And because ye are sons, <u>God hath sent forth the Spirit of his Son into your hearts</u>, crying, Abba, Father. (Galatians 4:6).

However, the baptism in the Holy Spirit is a separate and free gift to all who believe.

1 In my former book, Theophilus, I wrote about all that Jesus began to do and to teach   2 until the day he was taken up to heaven, after giving instructions through the Holy Spirit to the apostles he had chosen. 3 After his suffering, he showed himself to these men and gave many convincing proofs that he was alive. He appeared to them over a period of forty days and spoke about the kingdom of God. On one occasion, while he was eating with them, he gave them this command: Do not leave Jerusalem, but wait for the gift my Father promised, which you have heard me speak about. <u>For John baptized with water, but in a few days you will be baptized with the Holy Spirit.</u> But you will receive power when the Holy Spirit comes on you; and you will be my witnesses in Jerusalem, and in all Judea and Samaria, and to the ends of the earth. (Acts 1:1-8)

1And when the day of Pentecost was fully come, they were all with one accord in one place. 2And suddenly there came a sound from heaven as of a rushing mighty wind, and it filled all the house where they were sitting. 3And there appeared unto them cloven tongues like as of fire, and it sat upon each of them. <u>*⁴And they were all filled with the Holy Ghost, and began to speak with other tongues, as the Spirit gave them utterance. (Acts 2:1-4)*</u>

Here are some other scriptures that confirm that the baptism in the Holy Spirit is separate from water baptism:

⁸I indeed have baptized you with water: but he shall baptize you with the Holy Ghost. (Mark 1:8).

For John truly baptized with water; but ye shall be baptized with the Holy Ghost not many days hence. (Acts 1:5).

Then Peter said unto them, Repent, and be baptized every one of you in the name of Jesus Christ for the remission of sins, and ye shall receive the gift of the Holy Ghost. (Acts 2:38)

Then remembered I the word of the Lord, how that he said, John indeed baptized with water; but ye shall be baptized with the Holy Ghost. (Acts 11:16).

This man was instructed in the way of the Lord; and being fervent in the spirit, he spake and taught diligently the things of the Lord, knowing only the baptism of John. (Acts 18:25).

David and I quoted the same scriptures I have listed here for you. If you have not yet been saved or born again or received the baptism in the Holy Spirit and you would like to, simply pray this prayer with me now:

> Father God,
>
> I come to you and ask you to forgive all of my sins. I am asking you now to come into my heart and become the Lord of my life. I repent for every sin and renounce all ties I have had with demonic spirits, witchcraft or horoscopes. I also break every ungodly soul ties that I have with anyone and ask you to help me to stay free. I forgive every person who has ever hurt or offended me because you have forgiven me. I forgive myself for all of my sins and past failures. Your Word says that you cast all of my sin into the seas of forgetfulness and you cannot even remember my sin any longer so therefore, I chose to forget my sins and will not dwell on the past after this prayer. By faith, I ask you to baptize me in the precious Holy Spirit and give me the faith to receive the gift of tongues. Help me to serve you all the days of the rest of my life. Show me your plan for my life and lead me every step of the way.
>
> In Jesus Name.

Sign your name with today's date on your birth certificate.

❦

The word says:

⁹That if thou shalt confess with thy mouth the Lord Jesus, and shalt believe in thine heart that God hath raised him from the dead, <u>thou shalt be saved.</u> (Romans 10:9).

If you sincerely prayed that prayer, then the Bible clearly says that you have now been saved, born again. Your name is written down in the Lamb's book of life. You have the assurance that if you died today, you would go to heaven. The only way we can have a guarantee that we can make it into heaven is by the precious blood of Jesus. There is no other name under heaven whereby we can be saved.

¹²Neither is there salvation in any other: for there is none other name under heaven given among men, whereby we must be saved. (Acts 4:12).

You may not "feel" saved after you prayed the prayer but remember that our salvation is not based upon feelings but by faith.

⁸For by grace are ye saved through faith; and that not of yourselves: it is the gift of God: (Ephesians 2:8).

I remember when I was praying for my brother when he was in his twenties. I would pray for him to be under conviction of his sin. I would "shoot" prayers at him every time I would see him working in construction in our neighborhood. He didn't know that I was praying like that when I would see him as I drove by but soon after he came over to our house. He was under conviction of his sin and was crying. I knew in my heart he was ready to get saved so I asked him if he wanted to pray with me. He immediately said, "Yes." He was gloriously saved and wanted to tell everyone he knew about his decision

A few weeks later, he came over and told me he didn't "feel" saved anymore because he was still cussing and doing some of the same old sin he had before. I told him that he was not saved by feelings but by faith and I asked him again if he sincerely meant that prayer when we prayed. He said, "Yes." Then I explained to him that *God never leaves us nor forsakes us and that nothing shall separate us from the love of God. (Hebrews 13:5, Romans 8:35-39).* I then told him he needed the baptism of the Holy Spirit in order to have more power to overcome his weaknesses and break old habits. He quickly agreed and was ready to pray with me. I told him simply to ask God to baptize him in the Holy Spirit and wait upon Him to give him his prayer language or the tongues. I also told him to expect to receive and by faith to open his mouth and speak whatever word or words the Spirit gave him. In just a few minutes, he began to speak out the most beautiful words that sounded like, "Tee selah, tee selah." Then I told him to continue to pray in English and then pray in tongues every day. It takes faith to pray in tongues because you don't have any idea what you are saying.For he that speaketh in an unknown tongue speaketh not unto men, but unto God: for no man understandeth him; howbeit in the spirit he speaketh mysteries. [4]He that speaketh in an unknown tongue edifieth him-self. Edify means that when you pray in tongues you build yourself up. Not in a negative light, like pride, but in the sense of building a home. We need to build up our faith and our understanding by praying in tongues.

There have been several people, who have actu-ally recorded themselves as they prayed in tongues and then they sent their recordings to several differ-ent linguist specialists at various universities. They have heard back from these specialists and been told they were praying in old ancient languages. Although we cannot understand what we are praying, the Holy Spirit is giving us utterance and He bypasses our natural understanding and prays according to the perfect will of God. Now, wait upon the Lord in a quiet place and believe you receive the tongues. You may think in your mind that you are making up the language or that you only have one syllable that sounds like gibberish, but by faith, speak out that one word or words that come to your mind. God will not open your mouth and force you to speak in tongues.

If a son shall ask bread of any of you that is a father, will he give him a stone? or if he ask a fish, will he for a fish give him a serpent? [13]If ye then, being evil, know how to give good gifts unto your children: how much more shall your heavenly Father give the Holy Spirit to them that ask him? (Luke 11:11, 13).

You must exercise faith when you want to receive the baptism of the Holy Spirit and the tongues. The way that I received my healing was to stand on God's word. My healing first began when I started praying to forgive myself. It was a process that the Holy Spirit began by showing me how I talked to myself.

I would verbally beat myself up several times a day. You would be surprised if you could see a print out of your thought life on paper at the end of every day. I did not realize how much self-hatred I had neither did I realize how much these toxic thoughts were causing me to suffer from depression. As the Holy Spirit showed me these things, one-by-one, I began to confess and repent. I would tell the Lord that I forgave myself for such and such a sin and then tell Him that I am not going to dwell on that thought ever again. I began commanding the enemy to remove the self-condemnation and I would tell the Lord that His blood covered that sin and I would no longer beat myself up over that. If I needed to write someone and apologize, I did that too. Whatever I needed to do in order to gain peaceful thoughts that would I do. This went on for days. Just because you forgive yourself and go through the process of forgiving yourself, don't think you will never think of them again. You have to re-train your brain by standing on the Word.

Casting down imaginations, and every high thing that exalteth itself against the knowledge of God, and bringing into captivity every thought to the obedience of Christ. (2 Cor: 10:5)

When I would begin to think about my past sins or failures I would begin to quote this scripture along with many others I am going to share with you. You may ask,

"Out loud?" Yes, out loud and silently and many times with my husband or another prayer partner that I knew would agree with me for my healing. Another scripture that we would stand on is

Thou shalt also decree a thing, and it shall be established unto thee: and the light shall shine upon thy ways. (Job 22:28).

Most Christians do not have a clue about their inheritance and authority as a Believer. They think that salvation means that they have been forgiven from their sins and they can now enter heaven once they die. But beloved, salvation is much deeper than that as wonderful as that is. It would be enough if Jesus just died for our sins but He also took those 39 stripes for our healing.

The Greek word for save is "sozo". This word's origin comes from the word "safe". If you ever have any doubt that God wants you well, read this over and over and meditate on these words. They are your title deed, your inheritance, because of what Jesus did for you. He went all the way for us so that we can enjoy the abundant life.

Who his own self bare our sins in his own body on the tree, that we, being dead to sins, should live unto righteousness: by whose stripes ye were HEALED. (1 Peter 2:24).

When Jesus was being beaten unmercifully prior to the crucifixion, his back was lacerated by the scourging that took place. When Jesus was scourged, his hands and arms were out stretched and tied with cords on a frame. He was beaten with a handle that consisted of three pieces of leather or cord. Usually metal or bone was fastened to the cords. The Roman law was that you could not beat a person over 40 times because it would result in death so they usually stopped at 39. The scourging alone would have left Jesus in excruciating pain, not to mention the fact that he had been up all night without any rest or sleep and it is written that they plucked out his beard and spat upon his face. He was barely able to stand because of the tremendous loss of blood. That is why he fell under the weight of the cross as he walked down the Via Dolorosa (Way of Sorrows) where he was hung on Golgotha's hill. This was done for you and me, not for himself.

But he was wounded for our transgressions; he was bruised for our iniquities: the chastisement of our peace was upon him; and with his stripes we are healed. (Isaiah 53:5).

When you need healing, stand on these scriptures and remind yourself over and over what Jesus did for you. Put your name in the scripture and tell the demons of hell they have no authority over you any more because you are a believer, a child of God, and His blood never loses its power.

Take communion. There is healing in communion. In fact, I recommend that you take it often. I have heard of several people who were healed right after they took communion. I had been suffering for over a year from horrible withdrawal symptoms from getting off the Lexipro. My husband and I went to see my brother and his family in North Carolina and we all took communion together. I never had another bout with the withdrawal symptoms. Those emblems represent what Jesus Christ did for us on the cross and we are to take communion in remembrance of what he did for us.

And when he had given thanks, he brake it, and said, Take, eat: <u>this is my body, which is broken for you: this do in remembrance of me. (1</u> Corinthians 11:24)

There is an old hymn that goes:

Jesus paid it all, all to him I owe.

Sin had left a crimson stain; He washed it white as snow.

It is finished and Jesus Christ is Lord. Declare and decree that you are whole, healed, saved and delivered.

No weapon that is formed against thee shall prosper; and every tongue that shall rise against thee in judgment thou shalt condemn. This is the heritage of the servants of the LORD, and their righteousness is of me, saith the LORD. (Isaiah 54:17).

Learn to use your authority in Christ and your weaponry.

Then he called his twelve disciples together, and gave them power and authority over all devils, and to cure diseases. And he sent them to preach the Kingdome of God, and to heal the sick. (Luke 9:1)

Behold, I give unto you POWER to tread on serpents and scorpions, and OVER ALL THE POWER OF THE ENEMY: and nothing shall BY ANY MEANS HURT YOU. (Luke 10:19).

ALL POWER is given unto me in heaven and in earth. Go ye therefore… (Matthew 28:18:19).

Greater is he that is in you, than he that is in the world. (1 JOHN 4:4).

We are MORE THAN CONQUERORS through him that loved us. (Romans 8:37)

Neither give place to the devil. (Ephesians 4:27).

You may be thinking, well that was back then when the disciples were alive but how do I know that this healing still applies for today? Good question.

Jesus Christ *the same yesterday*, and to day, and for ever. (*Hebrews 13:8).* For ever, O LORD, thy word is *settled in heaven.* (Psalms 119:89)

What is my weaponry?

For we wrestle not against flesh and blood, but against principalities, against powers, against the rulers of the darkness of this world, against spiritual wickedness in high places. (Ephesians 6:12).

Resist the devil and he will flee from you. (*JAMES 4:7).*

You will come up against doubt and unbelief. These are the mighty weapons the enemy will use the most to keep you in bondage to sin, sickness or poverty but Greater is He that is in you, than he that is in world.

4Ye are of God, little children, and have overcome them: because greater is he that is in you, than he that is in the world. (1 John 4:4).

You are engaged in spiritual warfare but you have everything you need to win the battle if you are a Christian. God has supplied us with the amour.

10Finally, my brethren, be strong in the Lord, and in the power of his might. 11Put on the whole amour of God, that ye may be able to stand against the wiles of the devil. 12For we wrestle not against flesh and blood, but against principalities, against powers, against the rulers of the darkness of this world, against spiritual wickedness in high places. [13]Wherefore take unto you the whole armour of God, that ye may be able to withstand in the evil day, and having done all, to stand. [14]Stand therefore, having your loins girt about with truth, and having on the breastplate of righteousness; [15]And your feet shod with the preparation of the gospel of peace; [16]Above all, taking the shield of faith, wherewith ye shall be able to quench all the fiery darts of the wicked. [17]And take the helmet of salvation, and the sword of the Spirit, which is the word of God: [18]Praying always with all prayer and supplication in the Spirit, and watching thereunto with all perseverance and supplication for all saints; (Ephesians 6:10-18)

Years ago, in October of 1981, God showed me a vision. He told me that he was going to unlock the chains that held me captive and he was going to pull me out of the valley of depression. Then He told me that I would reach my hand down and pull others out of the valley of depression from which I had come. I believe this book is one of the ways God will use me to help others. I wish I had had this book so many years ago. Perhaps I would not have suffered for so long. God showed me there is a time to heal and He makes everything beautiful in his time.

To everything there is a season….A time to kill, and a time to heal; a time to break down, and a time to build up; (Ecclesiastes 3:3)

[11]*He hath made every thing beautiful in his time: also he hath set the world in their heart, so that no man can find out the work that God maketh from the beginning to the end. (Ecclesiates 3:11)*

CHAPTER 21:

❦

UPDATE! FINALLY MED FREE!!!

I have some exciting news! I began to have kidney problems which resulted in having frequent urination—so much so that I had to go to the emergency room which in turn led me to a urologist. He discovered that the Lithium Carbonate (LC) was causing problems with my creatinine levels. I eventually switched to Lithium Orotate (LO) a natural form of lithium, but still had problems. I was desperately looking for answers and prayerfully began to do a search on the internet for natural solutions for bipolar depression (bipolar type II).

I discovered a book by Aspen Morrow entitled, Med Free Bipolar: Thrive Naturally with the Med Free Method (Amazon). Aspen Morrow has the most amazing story of how she felt God led her to a product called Empowerplus by TRUEHOPE which enabled her to get off of all her medications for bipolar I, schizophrenic tendencies, ADD, anxiety and SPD.

TrueHope products were developed by Anthony Stephan and his friend after Anthony's wife, Debbie, committed suicide from suffering for years with horrible Bipolar Affective Disorder (BAD). Tragically, Debbie left him with 10 children. If losing his wife wasn't bad enough, Anthony began to notice two of his children were showing the signs of the disease and were also diagnosed with BAD. Anthony exhausted all medical help and was desperate to find answers. Through much prayer and research, these two men developed a program of nutritional supplementation that led to the recovery of Anthony's children and the formation of The Synergy Group of Canada Inc. This is a nonmedical research group entirely dedicated to the research of overcoming the disorders of the central nervous system. The hopeless picture of mental illness would change forever as a result of Debbie's tragic death and the determination of these two men destined to find a cure. They have found they have an 86% cure rate in their findings. There are testimonies as well as all kinds of information regarding the subject on their website www.truehope. com which I strongly recommend you visit and read first hand and the story of Anthony Stephan.

I called the Micronutrient Support at TrueHope and found the coaches were extremely knowledgeable and helpful. The coach gave me a plan to get me completely off of the Lithium Orotate (LO). She told me that a healthy brain will not need Lithium Orotate (LO), but would just need continuing feeding of nutrients, just as a car cannot run without gasoline. So with the help of their counselors, the journey began by cutting my Lithium Orotate by 1/16th. I was on 480 mg. daily. The weaning process took me about 10 months, but today, I can say that I am completely free of all medications with the exception of my thyroid medications.

During the weaning process, I was advised to take their Amino Acids product, AminoPower Advanced Veggie Caps, which helped curb the withdrawals tremendously; mainly, depression and fatigue. Sometimes in the beginning I would have to take 4 every hour to ward off depression.Eventually, it got easier to make the cut until I was completely off of the Lithium Orotate. My kidneys got so much better and I lost 30 lbs. No longer did I have to go to the bathroom every hour; I could get a good night's rest.

EVEN MORE GOOD NEWS! I later learned that I could get the Empowerplus96 & Aminos less expensively through the affiliate program through QSciences. I have hopes of earning my product free from them soon to help cover my own vitamins. So, if you decide to check them out, please use my affiliate link:

www.cherylvanwinkle.myqsciences.com &

www.micronutrientsupport.com   (micronutrient support is $35 per year if a QSciences' customer).

I now have a calm, coping and clarity I never thought I would enjoy again, and God is opening new doors for me to share my testimony. He has assured me that He would catch me when I jumped, and every door that I try to open on my own was being shut. God told me, "You don't have to try to push the door down; I am a gentleman, and I will open the door for you." I am seeking God for the next steps to take in this incredible, long journey into wholeness. God could have instantly healed me as he has so many, but He wanted to go deeper and heal me from the inside out--beginning with learning how to love and forgive myself, others and then trust Him to complete the work He began.

Philippians 1:6 NIV

Being confident of this, that he who began a good work in you will carry it on to completion until the day of Christ Jesus.

I hope my story has inspired and encouraged you. Many may say I am just trying to sell products but God knows I only want to help others find a cure for their depression and mental illness. I only wish I would have discovered this all the many years ago when I had to watch my mother and grandmother go through the horrors of shock therapy and endless trials of antidepressants. I thank my God every day for giving true and lasting hope and joy, and a reason to get out of bed every morning. God uses prayer, medical science and godly counsel to help us find healing. A merry heart does good like a medicine. (Proverbs 17:22). You don't have to feel depressed any longer, there is a better way. I pray that whatever reason you are suffering from depression that you will find your answer to find wholeness and freedom.

My book is available on Amazon.

If you are interested in having me speak at your church or womens groups please contact me at:

cherylbvanwinkle@gmail.com

Never give up hope for your healing!!!

www.ingramcontent.com/pod-product-compliance
Lightning Source LLC
Chambersburg PA
CBHW072131270326
41931CB00010B/1724